LEADERS

LEADERS

GARDNER M. NASON

SAY WHAT YOU MEAN, MEAN WHAT YOU SAY

ARCHWAY
PUBLISHING

Interior Image Credit: Laura Napolitano, Jim Bradshaw

Archway Publishing books may be ordered through booksellers or by contacting:

Archway Publishing
1663 Liberty Drive
Bloomington, IN 47403
www.archwaypublishing.com
1 (888) 242-5904

ISBN: 978-1-4808-7186-1 (sc)
ISBN: 978-1-4808-7185-4 (hc)
ISBN: 978-1-4808-7187-8 (e)

Library of Congress Control Number: 2019931289

Print information available on the last page.

Archway Publishing rev. date: 01/30/2019

This work is dedicated to
Jean, David and Nick.

ACKNOWLEDGEMENTS

Leaders: Say What You Mean, Mean What You Say is an amalgamation of what started at home, developed in my schooling, and observations, successes and failures experienced during a 40-year career in a variety of environments. In all of this, there were people every step of the way helping me. To attempt to name them all would be futile and an injustice to those not named.

Even so, I must name my parents – Gardner and Alice Nason. It all began with them. They did a great job raising five children, loving us, and making sure we had everything we needed. A sentence doesn't do justice to what they did for my brothers, sisters and me. The tragedy is they didn't live long enough to enjoy their golden years or see what they enabled.

Next, credit goes to all the teachers, instructors and professors at schools I attended – St. Joseph's in Garden City, N.Y., Chaminade High School in Mineola, N.Y., Norwich University in Northfield, Vt., and The Pennsylvania State University in State College, Pa. I was a late bloomer but ended strongly. Fortunately, my parents and teachers saw a glimmer of potential and didn't give-up on me until the maturity light turned on midway through my undergraduate years. For their faith and patience in allowing me to grow-up and find my niche, I am very grateful.

Additionally, I owe a debt of gratitude to the United States Army for sending me to Penn State for an advanced degree in journalism in a larger effort to improve relations between the media and the military. Also, for subsequent assignments (the Defense Information School, *SOLDIERS* magazine, the Army's Personnel Center, the 82nd Airborne Division, and the Communications and Electronics Command) that gave me the experience and confidence for success and satisfaction for the remainder of my time in the military and that served me well during a follow-on career in the private sector. I am grateful to countless soldiers of all ranks who cooperated and helped me, the Public Affairs community, and members of the civilian media whom I encountered and helped me help them. I benefited and learned from them all.

Post-military, age 42, and with marketable skills and experience, I landed as an account executive at Lanmark Group (now Lanmark360), a full-service marketing-communications agency in New Jersey with clients in dental pharmaceutics, equipment and related markets. At Lanmark, I gained experience working with copywriters, art directors, designers, illustrators, photographers and others all to satisfy client sales and marketing requirements. At the same time, I was a fly on the wall seeing what it takes to run a business – billing, meeting payroll, paying bills, hiring and firing, reworking and revising, delivering jobs, and competing for projects and new clients. It was eye-opening. I learned a lot from my friends and colleagues at Lanmark, especially from its principals, Christine Simpson and Joe Lancellotti.

Following Lanmark Group, I worked in information

-communications-marketing positions at Mount Olive College (now University of Mount Olive) in Mount Olive, N.C., aaiPharma (now AAIPharma Services Corp.), a contract research organization, in Wilmington, N.C., the Defense Information School at Fort Meade, Md., and Raytheon Company's Integrated Defense Systems in Tewksbury, Mass., and Washington, D.C. The common denominator at all these organizations was "telling a story" to audiences with specific interests whether it was internal or external, in a news release, ad, feature article, answering a media inquiry, doing interviews, preparing an executive for an interview, or offering counsel on how to deal with a dicey situation. In these positions, I had the good fortune of working with professionals and colleagues who were very good at their jobs and supported me in what I did. To all of them, I owe a "thank you."

In preparing this work for publication, I am indebted to friends who nudged me along the way – "Where are you now?" What should have been written in six months took five years of starts and stops, rewriting, changes, additions and editing. Writers know the drill. But in the end, it was Ellen Surles who gave my writings form, Laura Napolitano who prepared the manuscript for submission, Jim Bradshaw who polished the graphics that Laura roughed out from my chicken scratches on paper, and finally, the editorial staff at Archway Publishing who took an amateur's work and made it into something professional and tangible. I could not have finished this work without their talents and help. A heart-felt thank you to all my partners in this endeavor.

CONTENTS

INTRODUCTION

This book is written for primarily for leaders, not the communicators on their staffs, although they might find a useful nugget here or there. From working for leaders for thirty years in various environments, including the military, education, an advertising and marketing agency, and medium and large corporations, I realized that many leaders, good as they are in their respective fields, didn't have a good grasp of the whom, how or why of communications, or of what counsel and support they should expect from the staff. Of course, some did. They were *naturals*—comfortably and ably connecting with the people around them and instinctively adapting to their level and interests. As a Communications professional, it was easy working with the *naturals*. But too many leaders had only a vague notion of what communications is all about. My purpose here is to familiarize these leaders with the range of activities, language, possibilities and impact that effective communications can have, making them better leaders, with the result of their organizations being better informed and achieving better results.

Experienced Communications professionals know much of what is here and could probably add a good deal more. Given a receptive leader and time, these communicators should be expected to bring their leaders up to speed in the realm of communications. But not all leaders are receptive. And because our world is operating at warp speed, the learning curve is often too slow. For the new executive leader, this discussion is a jump-start. It gives him or her a short course on how communications should function in organizations, and it provides the basis for a relationship and dialogue between the leader and the Communications staff.

When I suggest that a leader should do this or that, take it with a grain of salt. It's a suggestion, a concept, an idea—but only if it makes sense for a leader's situation. And if a Communications staff member is implementing any of these ideas *on behalf* of a leader, make sure it is done with the leader's knowledge, input and blessing.

There is nothing original in these pages. Everything included is conventional knowledge that I experienced. I took the liberty of cherry-picking from these experiences and observations, all of which are addressed in articles, books and textbooks on communications in a more scholarly fashion and in greater detail. I claim none of it as my own; rather, it's my subjective selection of what I think works and would be helpful to a new leader or a leader desiring to communicate more effectively.

When I refer to communications as a generic function, it is in lowercase. When I refer to it as a staff function, like Human Resources or Sales and Marketing, it is in uppercase. Presidents, vice presidents, commanders, directors, project managers, team leaders, and section leaders are all *leaders* in my mind, understanding that their authority and influence is scaled differently depending on the number of people involved and the organizational structures. Wherever you are on the ladder, the principles hold.

Finally, read on with the understanding that there's lots of wiggle room. Get the gist of what I'm trying to say, and then bend and shape it to fit your situation. If you have comments or feedback, I would very much like to hear from you. Good luck!

CHAPTER 1

COMMUNICATING
EFFECTIVELY MATTERS

Congratulations! You've proven you are very good at doing what you do, be it accounting, banking, chemistry, engineering, government service, managing, selling, servicing, educating, leading—whatever you did to earn your place. You made it to a position of leadership—maybe even to the proverbial corner office, the executive suite, inside the glass doors. You are a leader: president, vice president, commander, director, manager, project manager, dean, team leader – a person of standing, responsibility and influence in your organization. No doubt you deserve to be where you are for all the right reasons. You've worked hard, acquired knowledgeable, gotten results, developed vision, earned respect, and shown potential for achieving more. All of this has been recognized by the powers that be—the person or people who will determine your future. Now the scary part.

> "Your success and the success of the organization you lead depend on your ability to communicate effectively."

How effective you are from now on depends on how good you are at leading, teaching, influencing, coaching, cajoling, convincing, negotiating, selling, motivating and directing. If you are fortunate to be a naturally good communicator, relate well, instinctively know what's on people's minds, what motivates them, and what worries them, then your likelihood of being successful in this position and advancing further is very good. On the other hand, if you are not a gifted communicator—a natural—then your technical expertise, prior accomplishments, and hard work, commendable as they are, may not be enough to guarantee your continued advancement. Chances are you fall somewhere in the middle. Wherever you are, this discussion of communications will give you some new ideas to consider, help you understand the dynamics of the communication process, and provide tips for you to be an even more effective communicator. In doing so, it will help you be more successful achieving your personal and professional goals.

Looking Forward

As much as promotions are a reward for superior past performance, the people who promoted you are looking *forward* more than backward. They have expectations that you will improve your performance by virtue of your new authority and influence in your area of responsibility. They expect that you'll have greater influence over a larger number of people, that your methods and processes for getting things done will be more widely implemented, and that your work ethic, knowledge, dedication and example will inspire others—all with the effect of achieving better results. This can be more than a little daunting.

How are you going to do? However you fare, your understanding and use of communications will play a big part.

A Case for Communicating Effectively

Your success and the success of the organization you lead depend on your ability to communicate effectively. Consider:

- You can't do the job by yourself.[1] How are you going motivate those around and under you to do what needs to be done?
- Your staff, managers and employees must know what you are thinking. They can't read your mind. How will they know your goals and expectations if you don't communicate them clearly?
- If you expect your team to achieve your objectives, you must tell them what you want and give them the information and guidance they need in clear and achievable terms. Do your meetings have a clear purpose, or do those attending leave with different interpretations of what they think you mean?
- You now have more constituencies to satisfy. They are above and below you, in adjacent departments and divisions, and internal and external to your organization. They include many disciplines, each with slightly different needs and interests. Recognizing their varied perspectives, do you tailor your message to satisfy each?
- The organizations and universe in which we operate are more diverse than ever before. Are you sensitive to whether what you say and how you act resonate with or offend those close to you or your internal and external audiences?

- Competition in the marketplace is fierce. How do you distinguish, differentiate and position yourself, your organization, and your products and services as the best or preferred solution compared to your competitors?
- You will face naysayers, skeptics and critics every step of the way. Knowing this, do you anticipate their objections, craft responses, and address their concerns up front and head-on *before* they become obstacles or issues?
- In this social media environment in which everyone with a smartphone is a potential news source, how do you manage the flow of information internally and externally ensuring your organization's official position is accurately stated? Do you have a designated spokesperson and policies in place about who is authorized to speak for the organization? If so, are these policies known and enforced?
- Are you big enough to have a Communications director and staff? If so, are they getting timely and accurate information from you and your staff, and do you know what support and counsel you should be getting from them?
- Or are you a small organization in which you are your own spokesperson? Do you need guidelines and tips about with whom and how you should be communicating and how to respond to the media in difficult situations?

As you assume the mantle of leadership, these are some of the questions you should be asking yourself.

Nothing Beats Knowledge

This discussion offers suggestions about communications tools and techniques to help you navigate the wickets and minefields that leaders find themselves in from time-to-time. It's not a question *if*—rather, it's *when*. But understand that, as important as communicating effectively is, it's not the only skill you'll need to succeed. First and foremost, knowledge of your field is a critical element. You need to remain proficient—nay, *expert*—in your field. There is no greater asset you possess or compliment that your colleagues can confer on you, whether they like you or not, than "Nobody knows this business better than Sally or Sam (insert your name)!"

Knowledge also implies knowing the market, including the competition, and envisioning the future. Since we're all in business to make a living for ourselves and profits for our stakeholders, you must be able to convert your knowledge to something marketable—to solve a problem or provide a service or product that someone needs. Greater knowledge leads to greater vision. When you know more, you see more possibilities, and the possibilities you see lead to new opportunities. So, stay attuned to developments, and recognize when changes are occurring.

Resist getting caught up in the administrative minutiae that come along with being in a leadership position. It's baggage—a bottomless pit. Yes, it's important and must be done diligently, but it's also a distraction from focusing on and staying plugged into your core business. Do what you must, but use your staff and delegate—a good reason to have a top-notch deputy, administrative assistant and staff. Technical knowledge is what got you to where you are, so don't neglect it now. Don't sacrifice your edge. Even though your workday may be longer since you now have more responsibilities, make staying expert in your field a priority.

And a Little Luck Helps Too

In addition to knowledge and communicating effectively, having a little good luck helps now and then: being in the right place at the right time; market conditions being right for what you have to offer; deciding to move when you did; taking calculated risks—personal, financial, professional; getting along so well with the new boss. Some say you *make good luck* by how you perform predisposing yourself to good things happening. That's another way to look at luck. But I think we can agree that some people are fortunate to be blessed with good luck out of the clear blue sky. However it happens, luck is a good thing. Have the honesty and humility to admit that it's not just because you're so wonderful or such a great manager. Also, recognize that luck is a two-way street. We've all known people who have had incredible runs of bad luck too. Life isn't always fair.

What's Important

But this is about *communications,* not luck. Subsequent chapters will address principles, ideas and techniques that are intended to help you be a better leader by being a more effective communicator with an eye to making you more successful in achieving your goals. We'll discuss what you *as a leader* should know. We'll talk about:

- basics of leadership and ethics
- the principles and process of communications

- what body language communicates
- the importance of knowing your audiences
- your communications staff and what to expect from them
- communications strategy and planning
- internal employee communications
- traditional media and interview techniques
- digital and social media
- basics of branding and advertising
- maximizing trade shows
- speaking and listening
- crisis communications

Understanding and applying what's discussed here will help fill in some gaps in your communications skills or refine what you are already doing. Everybody and every situation are different. View what's here as a buffet—take what you need or what resonates, modify it, and make it work for you. Leave the rest. And it may be helpful to keep this discussion on aspects of communications handy as a reference to peruse from time-to-time or consult for a specific situation.

Leader's Takeaway

Communicating effectively is *how* you guide, motivate and direct your team to accomplish what needs to be done. It is not a panacea. You still have to be expert in your field, attuned to your market, deliver excellent service, have quality products, and be on time and on budget. Easy to say; harder to do. Accept that communicating well is going to make the process of accomplishing what you set out to do a lot easier. Let's get started.

CHAPTER 2

LEADERSHIP AND ETHICS

Inseparable: Leadership and Communications

Although we all depend on communications for socializing and maintaining relationships, *leaders* depend on communications as the way to influence others to a specific end. When we get into discussions of leadership and its characteristics, it's hard to distinguish whether we're talking about leadership or communication. The two are inextricably intertwined. In the end it doesn't really matter which is which.

> "Leading by example is a powerful way to communicate."

Consider how selected principles of leadership are communicated in helping leaders achieve positive outcomes, such as getting a desired response, achieving organizational goals, and enhancing respect between leader and follower.

Lead by Example

"Follow me and do as I do" is what lieutenants and sergeants in the military are taught about leadership at its elemental level. In other words, follow the leader's example. The principle applies to leaders in all walks of life. How you behave and what you do in all aspects of your behavior communicate more than anything you say. Your peers, employees and subordinates observe your behavior and habits, and they take cues on what is acceptable. So do your children. Leading by example is a powerful way to communicate.

"Do as I say" doesn't cut it just because you're the boss issuing a directive unless you demonstrate that you also "walk the talk." The new person who walks in and takes over the position as the person in charge—president, vice president, director, commander, manager, department head, team leader—whatever level—commands respect initially by virtue of his or her title and position—but not for long. That respect, and the support that goes along with it, is quickly reinforced or eroded by how you act and what you do as soon as you take control, hold meetings, make decisions, and start to direct. Your knowledge, behavior and leadership style are evaluated consciously and unconsciously by those around you and are reflected in the support you get.

Leading by example is also wide-ranging. Your work patterns and habits are observed. It includes how you dress; when you arrive at work and depart; your stated view on work and home life balance compared to your observed work pattern; how you conduct meetings; your attentiveness when listening; your reaction to bad news and disagreeing views; how you address people; if you make eye contact; if you ever smile or laugh. In these circumstances and others, your example communicates the type of leader you are. Subordinates take cues on nearly everything you do, and some even imitate your

behaviors. You're under a microscope. The higher you are in an organization, the more people are watching and the less privacy you have.

And it goes beyond the workplace. People notice you while traveling, in restaurants, while shopping, at school events, at the gym, when
you're jogging. When you are out and about, assume somebody out
there recognizes you—someone from work, a spouse of an employee,
a friend, a friend of a friend. The fact of the matter is, being a leader,
you've achieved celebrity status of sorts. It comes with the territory.[2]
People are not deliberately spying on you, so don't be paranoid—just
be aware and behave appropriately.

As an aside, isn't it amazing to see individuals at the highest levels
of government, top executives in industry, high-ranking officers in the
military, entertainment figures, athletes—people in the spotlight and
positions of power—who think they can get away with illegal, scan-
dalous, unacceptable, or just plain bad behavior? Their judgment is
clouded by lack of awareness, greed, lust, power, arrogance—who knows
what? In behaving badly, they are abusing their position and authority.
Denying bad behavior or brushing it off as *only kidding, just having a
little fun, lighten up, it didn't happen like that, was misunderstood, was
taken out of context,* or *she's too sensitive* does not fly. They fool only
themselves. Don't be one of *them.* Most people—your employees, your
peers, even your children—have pretty good instincts about behavior.
They know what's right, what isn't, and if something smells fishy.

Your good reputation is a valuable asset. It takes a long time to
earn, yet it can unravel very quickly. Don't be careless or tempted to
do something you shouldn't. Why? First, because it's not right. You
know better, or should. Demonstrate the good sense to recognize
temptation for what it is. Second, because someone out there, somehow, somewhere, is observing and taking it in. And third, it will affect
your effectiveness as a leader. Your actions are seen, even when you

don't realize it. How you act communicates more than you realize and, for better or worse, affects your ability to influence others.

Tell the Truth

"Speak the truth" goes without saying, or should. Nothing will undermine your credibility as a leader quicker than not telling the truth. If you think you are the only one who knows the whole truth or what the real story is, you are not being realistic. Or, if you are, somehow, some way, perhaps later, the actual truth will come to light. Either way, if you are not truthful, you lose.

Also, leaders hurt themselves when they don't tell the complete truth, or when they obscure or sugarcoat the truth to a point where it's hard to figure out just what is being said. Don't mince words. Don't be ambiguous. Granted, there are situations that require confidentiality and discretion. When you cannot address a situation or answer a question that is screaming for a comment, at least explain why. For the most part, people know the rules when there are privacy, legal, security, or propriety considerations, and they expect you to play by them.

A *sin of omission* is just as bad as a *sin of commission*. Omission is a deliberate attempt to avoid or bypass the truth or not do what is supposed to be done. It gives the impression you are not aware, not informed, not attuned, or pretending a situation doesn't exist, equating to sticking your head in the sand. Again, you lose. Assume someone else knows what you are omitting. Inevitably, the complete story will come out. However the full details are eventually revealed, your decision not to be fully forthcoming undermines your credibility. So does stonewalling. Saying "No comment" or refusing to talk about a situation is not an acceptable response by itself. When you cannot comment or answer a question, explain why. Anticipate these situations and craft an explanation—something along the lines of these examples:

- "I know you are curious about Bob's sudden departure. I cannot share details except to say we had differences of opinion about how things should operate (or acceptable behavior) that could not be reconciled. I thanked Bob for his service here and wished him well in his future pursuits."
- "I know you are concerned about the rumor of a layoff. In this economy, anything is possible. Layoffs are on the table as we evaluate courses of action to keep the company viable in these challenging times. As soon as I know and am authorized to tell you, I will." (Be sure to deliver on your promise.)
- "I know that you are aware that Internal Affairs is conducting an investigation about unauthorized purchases (or the recent accident or pending litigation). Because it is an ongoing investigation, I don't want to say anything that might interfere or prejudice results. If you are questioned by Human Resources or an investigator, I encourage you to tell what you know honestly and completely so we can get to the bottom of it and get on with business."

Do not allow yourself to be in a position that conveys you are not facing the facts of a situation that falls within your purview.

Reveal Something of Yourself

Revealing something of yourself provides people around you with something to relate to. It gives them a connection or common ground for understanding you and your intentions.[3] People will be more willing to listen and follow your lead if they realize that you have something in common with them on a personal or professional level. This can be a little risky and should be done carefully to achieve a desired outcome.

Are you married? As appropriate opportunities present themselves, talk about your family. Superiors, peers and subordinates would be interested to know that you share the similar experiences and challenges as they do—good days and bad days, raising children, getting kids off to school, worrying about a son or daughter in college, a messy plumbing problem, getting the dog to the vet, going to your kids' soccer games—things that we all deal with in our day-to-day lives.

If you are single, gay, or divorced—whatever your state—same principle, different circumstances. You still have a life beyond the workplace. You have responsibilities, issues, challenges, hobbies, passions, favorite sports teams, movies, and authors, a book you are reading. Share a little of it. You decide what and how much. Prudently, people are protective of their personal lives. Nevertheless, sharing something of yourself reveals slices of humanity that bind us together.

Sharing something of yourself is good for relationship building, cuts down on speculation and rumors, and says something about your openness and honesty. It plows common ground for good communications. Demonstrating your humanity—likes, frustrations, passions, empathy—pays dividends in constructively connecting with the men and women around you.

Take Responsibility

Take responsibility for everything—the good and the bad—within your organization or span of control. It is easy to do when things are going well, but it requires character and guts when things go wrong. Don't make excuses, and don't shift the blame to others—"throwing someone under the bus"—especially subordinates. Whatever goes wrong in your organization, acknowledge it as *your* responsibility, and then proceed to fix it. If it was you who screwed up, stand up, be the man or woman, and take responsibility. If a subordinate in your organization caused the bad situation, stand up, be the leader, take responsibility, and then take the necessary steps to fix it. Even when things go wrong, you gain respect by how you respond. A big part of being a leader is being a problem solver. If you need to, get your smart people together and come up with an appropriately measured solution.

The process of arriving at a solution likely involves analytically and objectively investigating what went wrong—the facts of the matter, coming up with a plan to fix the problem, and then executing the remedy. It may result in process change, reaffirming that established and proven procedures are followed, equipment fixes or replacement, retraining or changing personnel—a host of possible actions. And the quicker the better within the resources and authority you have.

Reporting Bad News

Another aspect of leadership is reporting bad news. Report the situation to proper authorities (your boss, people whom the bad news affects, regulatory authorities) promptly, completely, and according to protocols. Like garbage, bad news stinks worse the longer it sits around. Don't make a bad situation worse by sitting on bad news. Beyond the bad news itself, delaying reporting reflects poorly on you, and it further delays fixing or remedying whatever went wrong.

No doubt about it, reporting bad news is unpleasant and takes courage. Hopefully, you work in an environment that doesn't "shoot the messenger," has a "we're all in this together" mentality, and marshals the resources to correct the situation, not repeat it or let others fall into the same unpleasant circumstance.

Respect Goes Two Ways

Everyone deserves respect. Showing respect is not the given it used to be. The leader who shows respect enhances his or her stature and, in doing so, amplifies his or her effectiveness. Regardless of position, people know when they are treated well. It's communicated in many ways—by what you say, how you say it, body language, consistency, sincerity.

Recognize that respect is a two-way street. Most people get the idea of respecting elders and superiors—upward, if you will—but don't always get the idea that respect also goes the other way—downward—to subordinates or to those junior to or younger than you. A leader who shows respect downward is not giving up anything or showing weakness. Rather, that leader is demonstrating maturity, sensitivity and recognition that everyone should be appropriately acknowledged and is a contributor in whatever the organization or endeavor is—and therefore is worthy of respect. Test yourself. Do you know the name of the person who cleans your office, workspace, or restroom, or anything about that person?

Sometimes the stress, negative news or the heat of the moment causes people to unhinge and forget respect. Guard against it. If you slip, go back and acknowledge the lapse to those concerned. "We were under a deadline. The boss was breathing down my neck. Customers were screaming for more product. I let it get to me. I apologize for reacting the way I did. Thank you for responding the way you did."

Try to stay cool in stressful situations. That's what leaders do, or should do. When everyone else is freaking out, you should be the one who is cool, calm and collected. If you stumble one time (oh, you're human?), promise yourself you won't let it get to you the next time.

Sometimes leaders are faced with unpleasant tasks, such as counseling someone for a violation or infraction or even dismissing an employee who deserves it. Even in these circumstances, take a moment to think through the situation and come up with a way to accomplish the dismissal, disciplinary or corrective action with respect and dignity. "I am sorry it has come to this. I have no other recourse. Thank you for all the good things you've done. Good luck to you."

How dismissals are conducted is often governed by Human Resources procedures. In many cases, it is unfortunate and unnecessary to see a dismissed employee escorted off the premises in the middle of the day in front of coworkers. It is embarrassing and humiliating for the now-former employee to be treated in this manner. If you can influence the action, do it at the end of the work day, on a Friday, or in such a way that minimizes the spectacle.

Of course, employee safety is a leader's responsibility. In extreme situations, swift and decisive action—having security or law enforcement authorities remove a threatening person—may be necessary. In these potentially dangerous situations, a leader's responsibility shifts from the offending person to protecting other employees or yourself.

Take Action

Morale in your organization can sometimes be adversely affected by a person who is not pulling his or her load, making mistakes, wasting time, or doing (or not doing) something that undermines efficiency, good order and discipline. In other words, there is a bad apple in the barrel. Often, peers see it and resent it but, for whatever reason—fear, lack of authority, not wanting to "rat" on someone, the offending person being intimidating or more senior—do not report it to a proper authority. Leaders need to be on the lookout for these kinds of situations and take action, whether it is counseling, retraining, a warning or dismissal.

Taking appropriate action is a leader's responsibility. It removes a negative influence, sends a positive message to others about acceptable and unacceptable behavior or work habits, and establishes consequences for what is unacceptable. "That person was getting away with murder for a long time. I'm so glad you acted," said or unsaid, is the response and effect a leader strives to achieve by taking action to maintain a healthy and productive work environment.

Be a Good Listener

Good listening is an important part of communicating *and* leading. Many opportunities are missed and mistakes made due to poor listening.[4] On the positive side, effective listening contributes to better relationships with those important to you personally and professionally. People want to know they are heard. Reasons for this include the respect it conveys, a human need for attention, a desire for empathetic hearing, and a sense of importance for communicating information. Effective listening is harder than it seems, requiring concentration and discipline, but it pays dividends to a leader. More in chapter 13.

Humility and Empathy

Humility is not the first attribute that jumps to mind when thinking of the qualities of a leader, but having a measure of it would serve a leader well. Not to diminish your personal qualities and achievements, but more than likely, you've had help from mentors encouraging you along the way, showing you the ropes, presenting you with opportunities, and advocating on your behalf. And now you are entrusted with people and responsibilities to run an organization or operation, a task you cannot do by yourself. You need the team as much as they need you. Acknowledge it. The success of an operation is in your hands, as are the morale, trust and livelihood of those who work for and with you.

Teachers in school *exist to serve their students,* equipping them with basic knowledge, social skills, a level of discipline, and the ability to reason, solve problems, and self-teach. Some students would argue that the opposite is true, and in a few cases, they wouldn't be wrong. In a sense, like teachers, leaders are given title, position, and authority to better serve their subordinates by providing them with guidance and direction, removing obstacles, and solving problems. In doing so, subordinates are better able to fulfill their responsibilities, which in turn helps the organization achieve its goals and objectives. Coming full circle, this ultimately reflects favorably on the leader. It's a matter of perspective.

Without being melodramatic, the trust and responsibility a leader shoulders both honor and humble the man or woman so fortunate to be in the leadership position. People depend on you, their leader. Remember what it was like coming up through the ranks as you looked to your leaders for guidance, encouragement, coaching, and honesty. Maybe you got what you needed; maybe you didn't but wished you had. Remember the good leaders. Now that you are in the position, make sure your subordinates are getting what they need. Ask them if it's not evident in other ways.

As you face and communicate with those in your charge, take opportunities to acknowledge and emphasize the team's importance, and do your best to create a "we're all in this together" and "none of us can do the job by ourselves" environment.

Be Generous with Praise and Rewards

Look for opportunities to praise and reward deserving people. They need to know their efforts are noticed and appreciated, and an acknowledgement goes a long way toward motivating that person and others to do more or achieve greater heights.[5] Bonuses, raises, and promotions are the ultimate highs on the praise and rewards scale, but money and pay are not the only ways to recognize a person's good work. A "nice job" from the boss can make a person's day and go a long way. Better yet, saying it in front of peers has an even greater effect. Other ways to communicate a "well done" include a personal note, a more formal letter included in the individual's personnel file, a framed certificate, a free lunch or gift certificate to a local restaurant, tickets to a movie, concert or sports event, a mention or round of applause at the next all-hands update … you get the idea.

Service awards (three years, five years, ten years, etc.) and retirements are other opportunities to honor the good work and loyalty of individuals in your organization. Make a fuss over these people. Depending on what you and your organization can reasonably do, hold an awards ceremony, banquet, luncheon or reception and encourage attendance. Invite spouses and significant others. If you have a manageable number of honorees, have a leader or the supervisor say something nice about each person's tenure and contributions. If there are many honorees, print a program that includes each person's picture with a nice write-up detailing his or her contributions.

Leadership is not a popularity contest. There is a job to be done and goals to be achieved. However, getting the job done and achieving the goals can be accomplished in an environment in which people respect their leader for all the right reasons, are well-informed, and know they are valued and respected.

Don't Be a Jerk

Don't be a difficult boss just for the sake of being tough. On the other hand, being regarded as a serious or strict boss with high standards is acceptable, even expected in most all environments, and is considered a desirable trait in a leader. People want to do a good job for a leader they respect, but it's hard to respect a person who leads by fear, intimidation or a desire just to assert authority because he or she can. Similarly, don't be the leader who seems forever unhappy, angry, contrary, critical or paranoid. Being an unpleasant leader creates unnecessary stress, discomfort and fear for everyone else in the workplace, and it diminishes the respect subordinates have for their leader in the long run.

Another test. When you happen upon a group of subordinates, are you greeted respectfully and engaged in appropriate work-related conversation, or with silence? Do people look your way or avoid eye contact? Do people smile or laugh in your presence? Do you ever smile or laugh in their presence? Look for ways to assess whether the people with whom you work display positive or negative body language or signals when you are present. These might be hints about how you are perceived.

Granted, personalities and leadership styles differ, and difficult situations call for serious and appropriate reactions that are sometimes unpleasant. It's okay to be angry or show displeasure with a situation or person so long as it's warranted and not a perpetual state. Life, business and the world around us run the gauntlet from good to bad to ugly and everything in between, and reacting is normal. Whatever your personality or leadership style is, strive to be thoughtful, reasonable and consistent as you deal with situations.

Ethics

Simple: *Be ethical.* Being ethical is doing the right thing routinely, but especially in dicey situations. There are general ethics, such as being truthful and putting in an honest day's work, and there are professional ethics, accepted and expected standards for those who work in a given profession or industry. If the rules you live by don't align with those of the people around you, there are going to be disconnects, confusion and problems about acceptable behavior and proper actions to be taken in certain situations.

Ethics are acquired in how we are raised, in what we learned from parents and teachers, in courses we took, in occupations we entered, in what we observe in the behavior of others, and in our own good and bad experiences. Ultimately, through amalgamation, ethics are formed and guide how we live and work.

It's not the intention of this discussion to say what your ethics should be, but rather that you recognize ethics exist, are important, are recognized and accepted, and are the standards that guide our actions when we are faced with difficult choices. Ethics are a moral compass and should override outside incongruent pressures, sometimes requiring courage and guts. They are analogous to rules of the road. Beyond the law, we all agree to drive on one side of the road and stop at red lights as reasonable and acceptable ways we all agree to and follow to avoid chaos, accidents and injury. Ethics are similar.

As a leader, it is a good idea to periodically mention ethics in a meeting, at an off-site retreat, annual sales meeting or planning conference, when addressing a large audience of people who are in your reporting chain, and when welcoming new employees. Talking about ethics sends a message that you recognize they are important, know ethical dilemmas arise in small and large ways in the work you do, and expect people to think, act and behave ethically in the work they do for you and your organization. Also, it implies that individuals in your organization can raise a question to a proper authority without fear of retribution when they are uncomfortable or not clear about the right course of action in a situation.

At the same time, don't unnecessarily dwell on ethics all the time implying there is a suspicion of issues, but rather raise the subject periodically and at appropriate times to let folks know ethics are always in the back of your mind and they serve as your underlying guiding principles. Be committed! Again, *walk the talk*. People somehow have very good instincts for distinguishing how committed we are about what we say, what we believe, and how we act.

It helps to write down your ethics, right along with the mission statement, purpose, objective, goals—however your business or organization states its *reason to be*—in the employee handbook and on the company's website. This provides employees with a ready reference and guiding principles for personal reflection should situations arise that are or have the potential to be an ethical dilemma. It's also good for customers, investors, and even competitors to see that you and your organization are committed to serving others according fair and just practices in how you operate. Besides showing you are on the side of *right*, it can also serve as a positive discriminator in your marketplace.

Finally, it is comforting for employees and subordinates to know they are working for an ethical leader and organization.[6] You know he or she will take the right action in a difficult situation. Conversely, it is very uncomfortable working for a boss or organization that doesn't demonstrate ethical behavior—not knowing what he or she will do in questionable situations that test character.

Leader's Takeaway

- Leading by example is powerful. Actions speak louder than words. Sound familiar? What you may not realize is, your actions are observed even when you don't think they are.
- Tell the truth. If you don't, you will be outed sooner or later and pay a price for it. If you cannot respond to a question or address a situation, explain why—whatever your reason.
- Share something about yourself to establish common ground—a bond—with the people you lead.
- Take responsibility for your actions and the actions of your subordinates. Don't make excuses. When things go wrong, fix them and move on.
- Be humble, generous with recognition, and don't be a jerk.
- Behave ethically and instill a sense for ethical behavior in your organization.

CHAPTER 3

PRINCIPLES AND PROCESS, VERBAL AND NONVERBAL

Principles and process form the basics of verbal communications. And then there is non-verbal communication—body language. By applying the principles, understanding the process, and exhibiting positive body language, a leader can become a better communicator and more effective in achieving desired results. Principles are guidelines—general in nature but widely accepted. Obvious as they are, principles are not always applied as matters of routine. Process is how human communication works—the mechanics. Body language works to reinforce or undermine what is being verbalized. This chapter elaborates on the importance of each. If a leader *gets* the principles and process of verbal and non-verbal communications—that is, sees, comprehends, understands, and applies them—then the rest of the discussion should fall into place as further elucidation or logical follow-ons to becoming a better communicator.

> "Your body language is either a fast ally or enemy very soon after you enter the room and start talking."

Principles

Principles are basic rules or guidelines that over time have proven to work. To be on solid ground, stick with them.

- **Say it clearly.** Say exactly what you mean, to preclude ambiguity or different interpretations. Use precise words and appropriate language stating your *intent* to provide clear guidance, especially in situations that require judgment and discretion.
- **Say it succinctly.** Fewer words are better than many. Say it in the shortest time or with the fewest words possible. The longer you speak or write, the greater the chance of the message or key points getting lost or your audience missing the point. When the subject matter is complicated and requires explanation, make your point succinctly and then elaborate.
- **Say it often.** Don't assume that because you said it once, it was heard and understood. Anyone who has children or a spouse afflicted with selective hearing knows this. Human nature is such that many of us need to hear information or guidance repeated before it penetrates and registers. Repetition is fundamental to learning. It imprints and reinforces. Also, in large organizations, never is everyone present to get the word at one time. Say it again—and again.
- **Say it honestly.** Listeners—receivers of your communications—can somehow look into your heart and determine whether you know what you are talking about and believe what you are saying. If you are not being honest, it will show.
- **Say it in multiple media.** People learn in different ways and get their information from different sources. For a message to get through and stick, some people need to hear it, while others need to read it. Some need both. With so many traditional, digital and social media channels and people's preferences and biases for

getting information, leaders need to employ as many different media channels as they have available. A one-time, one-way communication just doesn't do it.

- **Say it with emotion.** People respond to emotion. And it demonstrates that you have a personality and passion, react to good and bad, and are capable of glad and sad, light and serious, happy and mad. Expressing emotion evokes a reaction. Likewise, enthusiasm and passion—close cousins to emotion—are infectious and can be tremendous assets in persuading and influencing. Conversely, the lack of emotion or enthusiasm can be a death knell for any message or call to action.

- **Say it without notes.** If you can, talk it, don't read it. At least begin and end with good eye contact when speaking. It conveys, *"I'm talking to you!"* Good eye contact reinforces sincerity and confidence. Reading creates the impression of being scripted, and being scripted creates the impression of insincerity, being staged or lack of confidence. If your presentation is long, complicated or technical, of course notes and graphics are necessary. Even in these cases, start and finish looking squarely at your audience and speak from the heart. More on speaking later—in chapter 13.

When you think you have crafted a good message, before you transmit—by speaking, writing, publishing, broadcasting, emailing, whatever means you use—see how it stacks up against some of these principles for communicating effectively.

Process

When people communicate, a dynamic process is taking place. Understanding how the process works can help you communicate much more effectively and increase the probability that the message you are transmitting is received as you intended and gets the results you want. Think of the process as a loop. In *The Art of Public Speaking*, author Stephen Lucas describes the speech communication process. For purposes here, with slight variation, his model can be applied to all communications, not just public speaking. Lucas talks in terms of *speaker* and *listener*. Here, we use his model but substitute *sender* for *speaker* and *receiver* for *listener* of a message.

Lucas's communication process is comprised of seven elements: speaker (sender), message, channel, listener (receiver), interference, feedback, and situation. By understanding how each contributes to the process, you are likely to be more careful in how you approach communicating.[7]

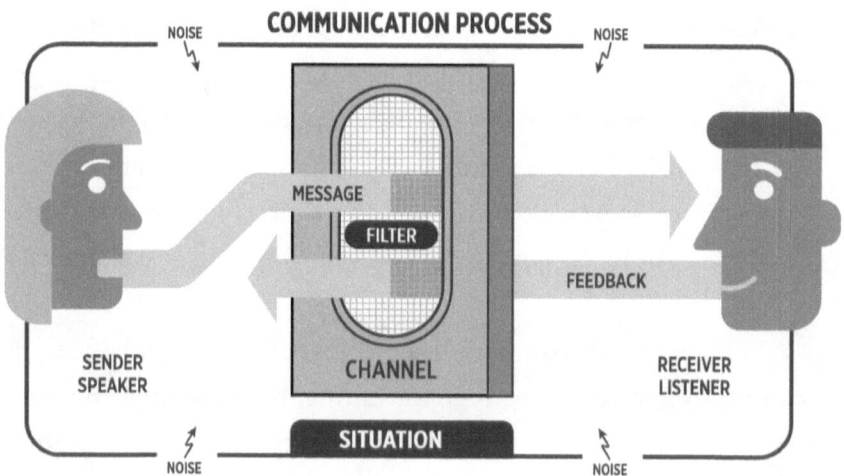

Elements of the Communication Process

- **Sender:** As a leader, you often initiate the communications process. In other words, you are the *sender*. Your success as sender depends on your ability to craft and transmit a message to your audience, whether it is one person or many, in such a manner that the message is received in a way you intended. Knowing your audience, using language they understand, and adapting the message to their interests all help you be an effective sender. Other factors, such as your position, reputation, credibility, motivation, and delivery, also have bearing on your effectiveness as sender.

- **Message:** The *message* is the content, the essence, the main point of what you intend to convey. It is the guts of what you have to say, however the message is transmitted.

- **Channel:** The *channel* is how the message is delivered—technically, mechanically. Channels include a face-to-face verbal conversation, talking with a small group, as in a meeting, speaking to a large audience from a podium with the aid of a sound system, using a telephone or mobile phone, broadcasting via radio, television, or webcasting, podcasting, blogging, and in print—letter, memorandum, and directives. The channel is the delivery vehicle—each with advantages and disadvantages. In person, face-to-face, is always best but not always possible or practical. Consider what *channels* are available to you, the importance of what you have to say, and consult your staff about which channel(s) to use. You may use one channel or end up sending or transmitting your message using several channels.

- **Receiver:** The *receiver* is the person or group to whom you, the sender, are directing the message. It is the person(s) whom you want to hear, see, read, understand and respond to what you say, write or broadcast. Communication does not take place unless there is a receiver. Just as a sender should adapt the message to his or her audience, a receiver also has a responsibility to listen, read, fight off distractions, and consider the message. Understand that a receiver receives a message filtered by his or her attitudes, prejudices, prior knowledge and self-interests regarding the sender and the message content.

- **Interference:** *Interference*, also referred to as *noise*, is anything that distracts or gets in the way of the sender transmitting a message to a receiver. Quite literally, it may be distracting noise in the hallway, traffic outside, or the hum of the air conditioning. Other forms of interference may be physical, such as an uncomfortable chair, a hot and stuffy room, a cold draft, or a poor sound system. And it can be psychological, such as a receiver's negative attitude or bias toward the sender or the message or a mental preoccupation with a family issue, another pressing business matter, or a wandering mind. The sender can also cause interference by speaking too long, in a monotone, or in a manner that doesn't connect with the audience.

- **Feedback:** *Feedback* is what makes the communication a two-way process. It is the mechanism that tells the sender if the message is getting through to the receiver and how it is being received. In providing feedback, a receiver becomes the sender, and the sender becomes the receiver. In a one-on-one conversation or a small group situation, a receiver indicates "I hear you," "I understand," "I agree," "I will do it" by looking at the speaker, head nodding, facial expression, and asking questions. When you are communicating with larger groups, recognizing feedback may be more challenging. The sender needs to work a little harder to interpret the eyes and faces in the audience, head nods indicating understanding or agreement, pertinent questions being asked. Sometimes, a speaker may stop midstream and ask point blank: "Am I making sense? Do you understand what I'm saying?" or invite questions. Negative feedback may be indicated by polite silence, loss of eye contact, no questions, restlessness, and attention shifting to out-of-sight cell phones. When indirect channels for communications are employed, there needs to be a feedback mechanism to give the sender an indication if and how the message was received. Failing to recognize the need for feedback and not providing for a feedback mechanism are common breakdowns when attempting to communicate.

- **Situation:** The *situation* is the circumstance of the communication. For communication to take place, the situation should be appropriate and conducive for the process to work. For a one-on-one conversation, privacy, proximity, familiarity and timing may be appropriate. For a small group, a comfortable, right-size meeting room on a subject or agenda of mutual interest creates a good situation. For a large audience, comfortable seating, a good sound system, and a comfortable temperature are called for. Periodic business reviews and updates are appropriate and expected from time-to-time. Should they be mandatory or optional? Good question—all part of the situation. Other factors affecting situation: if communicating digitally or via broadcast, does the entire audience have access to the channel to receive the message? Does the message contain good news or bad news? Is timing or the order of who receives your communique when important? Think about situation and endeavor to be appropriate in all aspects.

Learn the communications process; then make it part of your subconscious. Run everything you have to say through it. When you are communicating effectively, all the elements are accounted for and working. When you sense your message is not being received, or not in the manner you intended, then bring the communications process to a more conscious level and tick off the elements to see where the disconnect is.

Body Language

Body language reveals a lot about a leader's true feelings and motivation. Consequently, people tend to believe more what they see than what they hear. They do it unconsciously and quickly. One expert says that people evaluate a leader's credibility, confidence, likeability, and trustworthiness based on physical gestures, posture, facial expressions and eye contact in the first seven seconds of an encounter.[8] Another says people form their initial opinion of a person in less than four minutes. The point is that your body language is either a fast ally or enemy very soon after you enter the room and start talking.

Since credibility, confidence, likeability and trustworthiness are important attributes of leadership, paying attention to what you are communicating by how you move and present yourself can be as important as what you say. Depending on the signals your body is transmitting, you may be reinforcing or undermining what you are verbalizing, or sending mixed signals that are confusing, even contradictory.[9]

Much has been written about interpreting body language and how it affects communication between individuals and the effectiveness of leaders. This discussion merely touches the subject with the intention of making a few points. Body language matters because people make judgments about you based on what your body communicates. Whether you realize it or not, body language consistent with what you are saying adds emphasis, and body language inconsistent with what you are saying creates doubt and confusion, thus undermining your effectiveness. As a leader, you want your verbal and nonverbal transmissions to be congruent, one complementing and reinforcing the other.

Before we launch into this brief discussion, keep in mind a few cautionary notes:

- Body language is interpreted from the perspective of the eye of the beholder—the receiver, the listener, the audience.[10] Regardless of a leader's intent, why he or she consciously or unconsciously presented or gestured in a particular manner, what matters is how the body language was viewed, read and interpreted.
- A single gesture is not enough to arrive at a definitive conclusion. Instead, look for a few gestures or a pattern—*clusters,* in body language parlance—to validate a gut feeling before making a conclusion.[11]
- Consider the situation. People behave differently in different situations. A person's body language may differ in a casual social situation from that in a more serious business situation. Also, compare how the person acts and moves in particular situations to what you know is normal for him or her.[12] Personality is reflected in how a person acts, speaks, moves, and gestures—from goofy, casual and fun-loving to staid, serious and all-business—all affecting how the leader is regarded.
- The connotation of gestures differs among cultures.[13] The seemingly friendly gesture of "okay" or thumbs up in one culture can convey a very different meaning in another culture. Do your homework or get a coach familiar with nuances of

body language and customs if you have a culturally diverse audience or workforce or if you conduct business internationally.

What Your Body Language Communicates

With these cautions in mind, let's look at a few examples of body language and the reactions they elicit that may be helpful to leaders.

- Look the part—look like a leader.[14] For starters, maintain good posture, whether you are standing or sitting. Don't slouch or lean on your elbows on a table or at a podium. When sitting, lean forward, look at the person who is talking, and nod to indicate you are engaged, listening and interested. Leaning back or appearing too comfortable will have the opposite effect.
- Demonstrate confidence by standing up straight, head up and looking pleasant, feet comfortably apart, knees slightly flexed, weight centered in your lower body, all communicating a solid stance.[15] Let your arms hang naturally at your sides. Hold a book, folder or pen in one hand or the other if it makes you feel more comfortable. Avoid the "fig leaf" pose (hands clasped in front of the groin).
- When standing, try not to sway or shift weight from one foot to the other. Do not look down, and keep your hands away from your face or hair. These movements convey uncertainty or nervousness.
- Walk with a purposeful stride.[16] Your stride indicates you have a destination, a place you need to be, something you need to do. Don't walk looking at papers or your cell phone. As you pass people you know or recognize, acknowledge them with eye contact, a nod, or a hint of a smile if not a greeting.

- When appropriate, smile. Lighten up a bit and look for opportunities to smile. In *The Definitive Book of Body Language,* authors Allan and Barbara Pease say, "Smiling directly influences other people's attitudes and how they respond to you."[17] Furthermore, smiling is contagious. The normal reflex of the person to whom the smile is directed is to smile back, an effect known as *mirroring.* When you do smile, make it sincere, one in which your whole face lights up and your eyes crinkle.[18] If the situation allows, while smiling, say something pleasant, such as: "Yes! That's a great idea! Wish I'd thought of that! Nice going!" or "Good to see you again!" It's a good way to build and reinforce positive relationships.

- Eye contact is powerful. It indicates interest and is arresting in establishing a connection with another person. Our eyes keep returning to things that attract us—people and objects.[19] Eye contact not only connects, but also provides feedback. Much has been written about what eyes communicate compared to other examples of body language.

- Whatever the situation, assume open positions indicating inclusiveness, accessibility and collaboration. Face or square up with your head, torso and shoulders toward whomever you are speaking with, showing that he or she has your attention and interest. Looking sideways over your shoulder or turning away indicates little interest or disengagement.[20]

- Be aware that you are transmitting disagreement or defensiveness when your arms are folded, fists are clenched, wrist or arm is gripped, eyebrows are lowered, eyes are squinting, lips are compressed, or jaw muscles are tight, or when you are leaning back and looking away.[21]

- Remove barriers. Staying behind your desk, holding a brief-case, laptop, or purse, and even having a cell phone in view can diminish the quality of the connection a leader has with another person or an audience.[22] Put it down, move it aside, put it away, or reposition, demonstrating receptivity and openness. When speaking, a large podium and being on a stage too far away are other forms of barriers that work against a leader attempting to connect with an audience.

- Hands are revealing. Keep your hands in view, open and qui-et—a positive indication of interest. Showing palms is an indication of truth, honesty and willingness.[23] Hand gestures often indicate feelings, passions, appeals, and emphasis. A good speaker's hand gestures are naturally synchronized, emphasizing what he or she is saying. Hidden hands suggest hiding something, untrustworthiness, or a reluctance to participate. Finger pointing is a very annoying gesture; yet finger touching, such as steepling, signals confidence and authority.[24] Drumming fingers indicates boredom. Hands say a lot!

- Have a good, firm handshake. The intention is a friendly greeting. Be the initiator, and hold the other person's hand an extra second. Extend a vertical hand, and match the other person's grip.[25] Don't crush the person's hand, and don't offer a limp hand. Make eye contact, smile and start talking.

Closely related to body language is being conscious of a person's space—your space and the person's with whom you are communicating. An appropriate distance between individuals is largely determined by what is comfortable, considering the relationship between the individuals.[26] In the interest of a healthy and respectful work environment, everyone, leaders especially, is wise to recognize and adhere to spatial boundaries honoring a person's comfort level, maintaining mutual respect, protecting reputations, and not having gestures mis-interpreted or unwelcome liberties taken. In *The Silent Language of Leaders*, Goman suggests the following:

- *Any* physical contact, touching, or being closer than eigh-teen inches is reserved for loved ones—family and very dear friends.
- The close personal zone of eighteen inches to two feet is for friends, personal staff, and trusted colleagues.
- The far personal zone of two to four feet is for team members and business associates.
- The social zone is four to twelve feet for most professional dealings and new acquaintances.
- The public zone is over twelve feet.

Concluding this brief introduction to body language, don't under-estimate the importance of what gestures and movements communi-cate. Ideally, your body language naturally fits the context of what you are doing or saying. In other words, the verbal and nonverbal parts of your attempt to communicate are consistent and aligned with your intentions. The result reinforces your objective. On the other hand, if the words and actions don't seem to jibe or fit, then your audience senses something is wrong or not working and relies on what you are communicating nonverbally, diminishing or discounting your verbal message.[27] *He or she is saying one thing, but I'm not understanding or getting the right vibe. Something is not right. I cannot quite put my finger on it. I'm not convinced.*

If you are a good speaker, comfortable in your role, and confi-dent about what are talking about, then your body language tends to naturally complement your message. This is where you want to be. However, if you are a new leader or not completely comfortable in your role, then pay attention to how your body language may be reinforcing or undermining what you are saying. To improve, rehearse more, ask a trusted colleague to observe you and give you his or her impression, have your presentation videotaped to self-evaluate, or get a coach. Also, watch other people present with a critical eye, evaluating how their body language helps or hinders their presentation.

Leader's Takeaway

Humans have been communicating for a long time. By now—in the twenty-first century AD—we think we know how communications—both verbal and nonverbal—works. Be a tough critic in evaluating how well you adhere to communication principles, consider all elements in the communications process, and ensure that your body language is consistent with what you are saying.

- Apply the principles—say it clearly, succinctly, often, honestly, in multiple media, with emotion, and without notes.
- Communications is a dynamic process. Understanding the elements of the process will help make you a better communicator.
- Body language can help or hinder what you are trying to communicate. Strive for natural gestures and movements that are consistent with what you are verbalizing, and be conscious of gestures that are incongruent with your words that may confuse or cause doubt.

CHAPTER 4

YOUR AUDIENCES

One size, or rather one version, does not fit all when communicating. Who is *all?* Your audiences. Your audiences are diverse individuals, different in their interests, backgrounds and attitudes. Especially as a leader, the better you know your audiences, the better you can tailor your communiques—be they spoken, written, or digital—to achieve the results you want. When you tailor your message, the individuals in your audiences become more receptive to and interested in what you are attempting to communicate, and you are more likely to get the desired effect, whatever your reason for communicating.

> "The better you know your audiences, the better you can tailor your communiques to achieve the results you want."

Granted, communicating is a two-way process (chapter 3). The sender of the message and the receiver each have a role and a responsibility. In this chapter, we're asking you as leader and sender to be mindful of your audience and gear the message to the audience to achieve maximum effectiveness. Lucas refers to this as being *audience centered.*[28] Likewise, the audience—the receiver of the message—has a similar obligation to make a genuine effort to comprehend what is being transmitted, requiring them to pay attention, have an open mind, and resist distractions. More on listening in chapter 13.

Being audience centered means gearing the level or details of the content, language and delivery to the audience to achieve the best results—making the sender's point in a manner that the receiver(s) understands.[29] In others words, as a leader, you modify or tailor your approach as you communicate with floor and line workers, administrative staff, middle managers, technicians and professionals, and senior leadership, recognizing every level and department of your organization has different interests and questions. Not only will your communications be more effective, but also you are demonstrating respect for their perspective and concerns. We're not talking about *dumbing down*—rather, being audience centered to achieve the best results.

For Example

As an example of tailoring a message to the audience, think about your family for a moment. How you would inform members of your family that your elderly mother—your children's grandmother—has had a heart attack and is in serious condition in the hospital? Surely, your discussion with your spouse would be different from the conversation you would have with your fifteen-year-old daughter, and very different from the one you have with your six-year-old. As members of the family, they have a right to know what's happening, but each has a different capacity to understand, a different reaction, and different questions about the possible outcomes. Sensitive to these differences, you adapt what you say to each.

Another example: Imagine you are a scientist speaking to an audience of peers in your field about some exciting results of research you've been conducting. Speaking to fellow scientists, you can assume a baseline knowledge and familiarity with scientific language and concepts. Your presentation and the ensuing discussion will be at a high level, meaningful and appropriate for the audience. This audience wants to know about your research findings for their scientific implications and possible applications. However, a layman in the audience, a person without a scientific background, would likely not understand much of what you and your colleagues were talking about.

Same subject, different audience—you, the scientist, are now talking with investors. Surely, you recognize they are an important audience whose support is crucial for financing your work. In this situation, you would use terms and language they understand. You recognize their interest in your research findings is in their earning potential; therefore, you tailor your presentation to address their interests as investors.

Yet again, picture that you are talking to high school students who are on a science club field trip. Although you are talking to them about the same subject—your research—your approach would be very different from those you present to either scientists or investors. These high school students are interested in understanding the process or exploring career possibilities.

Another possible scenario: Competition in your business sector is becoming keener. It is clear to you that if your organization is to survive and remain competitive, significant changes will need to be made. As you think about presenting what actions will need to be taken by various groups within your organization, you are challenged to address what must be done to keep the organization viable and thriving based on how it will affect those who have vested interest in the organization and whose approval, support and help you will need to achieve the necessary changes.

The prospect of change unnerves many people, even though it is constant and necessary. This fear is largely driven by self-interest and the unknown. To minimize the anxiety that the mere mention of change will cause, a leader must anticipate, analyze and address the impact and concerns the changes will have on various groups inside and outside the organization.

To employees, their first concern is job security. They need be made aware that if change is not implemented, their jobs could be jeopardized. As changes are proposed, their buy-in and support are essential. Changes are likely to imply retraining, reconfiguring of the organization's structure, different requirements for certain skill sets, qualifications and experience, new equipment, different schedules, possibly automation or outsourcing—all unsettling to what people know to be business as usual.

In this situation, the smart leader anticipates these concerns, shows empathy, optimism and encouragement, and has answers to the extent possible or a least a plan for implementing the changes with the intention of allaying anxieties and building confidence. It is a situation calling for thoughtful preparation.

In each case, we're talking about being audience centered to achieve the best results. Your situations may not be nearly as dramatic as these. However, even for routine matters, you tailor your communication with the purpose of ensuring your audience gets the message with thoughtful consideration for their roles and interests.

Depending on what kind of an organization you are, while the objective may be the same, a leader may need to adapt his or her language, style and approach to the audience he or she is addressing. Even an organization's board of directors, investors, suppliers, current customers and other audiences will each have concerns based on their respective perspectives, relationships and self-interests.

Nothing New

The concept of understanding your audience is nothing new. Marketers, pollsters, consultants and analysts dissect, analyze, segment and label individuals and groups in every conceivable way to learn their preferences and tastes for the purpose of selling products, getting candidates elected, and steering a defined group to a decision or course of action. They slice and dice demographics to understand how each segment thinks, what they like, what buzzwords work, and what turns them off, all to achieve an objective—the same thing a leader should be doing when communicating with an audience.

Audiences = Publics

As a matter of semantics, *audiences* are referred to as *publics* (plural) among Communications and Public Relations professionals in recognition of the fact that there are many subgroups defined by interests, positions and relationships to you and your organization, as well as by the demographics of age, gender, sexual orientation, race, culture, education, economic status, political leanings, marital status, buying habits, attitudes, and other lifestyle preferences. You name it—there is a definable group, public or segment out there, often with statistically predictable tastes and biases.

Who Are Your Publics?

Who are the publics in your line of work? Depending on where you are in the leadership chain, your publics may include your board of directors, senior management, investors, stock- and stakeholders, middle management, supervisors, professionals, technical staff, line workers, people in Operations or Manufacturing, Human Resources, Finance, Sales and Marketing, administrative staff, cooks, maintenance workers, custodians … the list goes on to include their families, spouses, significant others, and even their children.

Another question: Do you have operations or people in multiple locations, different states, different parts of the country, and different countries? Sales, technical and service representatives scattered about? How might this wide distribution and diversity affect your approach and timing in your effort to be audience centered?

Not done yet—don't forget suppliers and contractors, your industry associations, trade and business media, and even your competitors.

Still not done—the community(ies) where your organization is located, where many of your employees live (including you), the local mayor, town council members, police and fire chiefs, and state and federal representatives.

It is not realistic to suggest that, as a leader, you should be communicating with all these publics all the time, but depending on what your organization does, how large it is, and what kind of an impact it has, either you or someone in your organization should be in contact with many of these publics at one time or another.

As part of your strategic and business planning cycle, it might be helpful to consider, even chart, all publics that affect your business or organization. Then assign a priority of importance, a frequency of how often you or a member of your staff should communicate with each, if at all, and how that communication or interaction should take place. A good project for your communications director!

Leader's Takeaway

- In communications, marketing and public relations circles, audience segments defined by demographics and preferences are referred to as *publics*.
- Endeavor to be *audience centered* in all your communications by tailoring your message content, language and approach to achieve optimum effectiveness with each definable public.
- Realize there are many publics who have interests in you and your organization, each for different reasons driven largely by self-interests. Use your staff to help anticipate, analyze and address the concerns of each public, deciding how important each is and how much energy and resources each deserves.

CHAPTER 5

STAFFING

Recognizing that every organization is different, suggestions here provide a starting point to build your organization's Communications capabilities by identifying functions and duties. Whether you are a large corporation with thousands of employees at multiple sites or a one-office business with ten employees, this chapter suggests the skills and qualifications your Communications lead and staff should have.

We live in a highly specialized world where the breadth of knowledge in every field has grown exponentially. The same holds true in Communications. Everything is more sophisticated, nuanced, complicated, and technical. In last fifty years, the media world has expanded from newspapers and magazines, broadcast radio and television, to broadcasting via cable and satellites, websites, blogs, social media platforms, podcasting, and streaming, with new and creative ways of utilizing each to inform and market. Advertising, public relations, community relations, crisis communications, and social media consulting have spun off into niche businesses—all with specialized agencies, boutiques and consultants offering counsel and advice or willing to do it for you on an outsource basis.

Also, Communications interacts with, overlaps, and depends on Human Resources, Sales and Marketing, Training, Safety, Security, and other departments for timely and relevant content, and they look to Communications for support in getting the word out. Drawing organizational charts with solid and dotted lines, agreeing on where departments intersect, who has primary responsibility, and when coordination and participation are necessary for efficient functioning can be challenging and complicated in any organization, especially in large organizations and corporations.

If you are serious about communicating effectively, have a Communications professional on your staff—and, if you can support it, a Communications staff to execute this critical function. Communications professionals should be keeping up with and effectively utilizing emerging technologies. In addition, they should be monitoring, evaluating and applying the ever-increasing body of research, analysis and case studies about what motivates people, how individuals and groups receive and process information, and what works in special situations. Having Communications professionals on staff who know the business, are knowledgeable about your organization, and are paying attention to the latest thinking and advancements can be a valuable asset.

However, if the Communications function is an *additional duty* for another officer, such as a vice president of Human Resources or Sales and Marketing, it stands a good chance of being secondary, an afterthought, reactive instead of proactive, and not done as well as the function deserves. The focus of communicating effectively could get lost or buried in the crush of everything else that needs to be done, resulting in you as a leader and your organization being less effective than you should be, and even hurt by it.

Traditionally, Communications departments are lean, and many are understaffed for the job that should be done. One reason is that many executives and staffing specialists don't see Communications as a revenue producer; therefore, the function is counted as overhead—a nice-to-have luxury. Another reason why Communications is often understaffed is that leaders do not understand potential benefits of a comprehensive and aggressive Communications program. They don't expect or require much, missing out on many contributions a well-staffed and functioning department could provide.

Done well, an effective Communications program contributes to an organization's success however you define it—achieving objectives or producing revenue, albeit indirectly. Most sales and contracts are not realized due to one sales visit, one pitch, one demonstration, one ad, one person's recommendation, one prior experience, or one visit at a trade show. Rather, it is a combination of your product's utility to fill a need, its quality, your service, your brand's track record, ease of doing business with your company—in other words, the collective efforts applied together consistently and over time that differentiate you and your organization from the competition. An effective Communications program directed continuously and consistently inside and outside your organization motivates, entices, tells your story, and makes your case on several levels. Don't underestimate the potential value of the Communications function and skimp on staffing.

What's in the Name?

Different organizations use different names, titles or labels to identify their Communications function, manager, office or department. When you look at what they do, often their duties and functions are similar. In deciding what works best for your organization, assign a title that is descriptive, inclusive and in line with your expectations. Whatever title the Communications carries, avoid having its function confused with Information Technology. Titles seen commonly on organizational charts include variations of the following:

- Corporate and Public Affairs
- Corporate Communications, or just Communications
- Marketing-Communications
- Public Affairs
- Public Relations
- Public Information
- Information

Positions and Responsibilities

Consider staff positions and responsibilities that are important to you to determine the right size of Communications support appropriate for your organization.

- Communications principal staff officer—vice president, director, manager
    - Responsible for developing and executing a communications strategy and plan that support the organization's mission objectives and/or business plan
    - Identifies publics important to the organization and develops a plan for engagement with each
    - Serves as advisor to the CEO, president and senior leaders of the organization with a seat at the table as a peer with other primary staff providing counsel and advice on internal and external communications matters

- o As needed, provides speechwriting, talking points, interview preparation, coaching, and critiques to senior executives
- o Ensures that all manner of internal and external messaging is consistent with organizational objectives
- o Maintains close working relationships with and provides mutual support to counterparts in Human Resources, Sales and Marketing, Investor Relations, and Legal departments, as well as project managers and other key players
- o Supervises and directs the Communications staff, performing related administrative responsibilities
- o Serves as the organization's spokesperson

- • External Communications (also Media Relations)—director, manager, lead
  - o Develops and executes the media relations plan that complements the organization's mission objectives and business plan
  - o Develops a list of media outlets important to the organization
  - o Identifies and establishes a rapport with key media players (reporters, editors, news directors, bloggers)
  - o Drafts, coordinates for approval, and distributes news releases
  - o Answers media inquiries with approved responses
  - o Identifies and coordinates other media opportunities, such as interviews, demonstrations, features, announcements, press briefings, editorial boards, tours

- Works closely with Information Technology and Digital, Social Media, Webmaster lead to ensure content and messaging on the website are aligned with the organization's business objectives
- Prepares and coaches leaders and subject matter experts for interviews, monitors during, and critiques after

- Internal (also Employee) Communications—director, manager, lead
    - Develops and executes internal and employee communications plan that complements the organization's mission objectives and business plan
    - Develops and manages internal channels for informing employees at all levels and locations, via intranet, newsletters, posters, local or closed-circuit television, and electronic and traditional bulletin boards
    - Makes sure channels flow information top down and bottom up
    - Maintains a close working relationship with counterparts in Human Resources, Security, Safety, Training, Pay and Benefits, and other functions, ensuring up-to-date and relevant news and content are available to employees
    - Constantly looks for opportunities to educate and reinforce organizational mission, priorities, policies and procedures to achieve efficiency, team building and good morale
    - Shares recognition about commendable service and accomplishments of employees and teams

- o In coordination with Human Resources, Security, Safety, and Information Technology, participates in a rapid notification system for emergency situations with contingency messaging and direction over primary and secondary channels

- Community Relations—director, manager, lead
    - o Develops and executes the community outreach plan that complements the organization's business plan
    - o Identifies and compiles contact information of key community players, including those in local, state and federal government, industry and professional associations
    - o Maintains an open line of communication and cooperation with local law enforcement, fire and rescue, and emergency medical services
    - o Researches, recommends and manages appropriate sponsorships, scholarships and volunteer opportunities
    - o Establishes and maintains a list of speakers, or manages a speaker's bureau when and if opportunities exist
    - o Serves as the liaison with community organizations and clubs, such as the Chamber of Commerce, United Way, Red Cross, Toastmasters, Special Olympics, civic, business and veterans groups, outing club, health fairs, running and walking events, holiday parades, etc.
    - o Manages protocol and courtesies for special visitors, facility tours, gift-giving, luncheons, banquets, flag placement

- Digital, Social Media, Webmaster—director, manager, lead
    - Develops and executes the digital and social media portion of the organization's business plan in coordination with Information Technology, Human Resources, Media Relations, and other interested players
    - Manages architecture and functionality of the organization's internal (intranet) and external (Internet) websites in close coordination and collaboration with Information Technology
    - Ensures up-to-date, relevant content on the organization's intranet and external website in close coordination with Employee Communications, Media Relations, Human Resources, Sales and Marketing, and other departments with interests
    - Manages and monitors the organization's policy and participation on selected websites, blogs and other digital outlets
    - Keeps leaders informed of relevant traffic, feedback and trendings
    - In close cooperation with Information Technology and Security, is vigilant of and acts to prevent interruptions from viruses and cyber threats
    - Identifies, recommends and facilitates opportunities for leaders to participate in dialogue on social media platforms

- Advertising and Trade Shows (together or separate)—director, manager, lead

o   Develops and executes advertising and trade show
    plans that complement the organization's mission ob-
    jectives and business plan

o   Maintains and monitors an up-to-date list of publi-
    cations, websites and trade shows important to the
    organization's line of business

o   Requests and maintains media kits (rate cards, edito-
    rial calendars and subscriber demographics) and trade
    show packets for relevant publications and events

o   Manages advertising and trade show budgets

o   Looks for and negotiates discounts, package deals and
    add-ons for multiple buys and participation

o   Serves as the primary point of contact with the orga-
    nization's agency for the development of advertising,
    trade show booth, graphics and displays, and other
    marketing materials

o   Coordinates closely with Sales and Marketing to en-
    sure advertising and trade show displays are consis-
    tent with business priorities and timing

o   Ensures that advertising, trade show displays and collat-
    eral marketing materials, such as literature, CDs, mem-
    ory sticks and giveaways comply with organizational
    branding, formatting, messaging and logo standards

o   Manages logistical support—shipping, setup and
    breakdown, utilities, labor, etc.—for participation at
    trade shows

o   Coordinates with Media Relations and Community
    Relations about opportunities for advertising, articles
    and interviews in trade show programs and dailies,
    hospitality suites, and social events.

- Graphics, Design, Media, Photographic and Audio-Visual Support—director, manager, lead
  - o Develops, maintains, disseminates and enforces a style guide consistent with organizational branding that governs standards for design and logo use, including signage, stationery and templates for presentation, i.e., all visual representations of the organization
  - o Serves as the organization's internal agency for graphics and design support
  - o Designs and prepares pre-press materials for commercial printing
  - o Coordinates printing with outside vendors
  - o Supervises video production, including technical support for planning, storyboarding, scripting, videotaping and editing, or coordinates with outside vendors
  - o Provides or supervises audio-visual support for meetings and events, or coordinates with outside vendors for support
  - o Recommends and manages a budget for graphics, design, media, printing and audio-visual support.

- Ancillary functions that are sometimes grouped under Communications include:
  - o Protocol—coordinates arrangements and courtesies for ceremonies, events and special visitors
  - o Librarian—maintains reference materials, resources and historical documents and records
  - o Historian—captures, preserves and catalogs organizational history, milestones and accomplishments

- o Printing—provides in-house printing and reproduction
- o Bands, vocal groups, demonstration teams, other forms of entertainment.

Merging and Right-Sizing

Many organizations cannot support a large Communications staff dedicated to the functions outlined above. Functions can be merged and tasks pared down to a manageable job description in any combination or configuration to what makes sense for an organization. One methodology is to organize into a predominance of *external* and *internal* responsibilities.

- External: Media Relations, Internet, Social Media, Community Relations, Advertising, Trade Shows, Protocol
- Internal: Employee Communications, Intranet, Branding, Graphic and Media Support, Printing, Librarian, Historian

RIGHT-SIZING

COMMUNICATIONS LEAD (VP, DIRECTOR, MANAGER)	
EXTERNAL DIRECTOR, MANAGER	**INTERNAL** DIRECTOR, MANAGER
Media Relations	Employee Communications
Website (Internet)	Intranet
Social Media	Branding
Community Relations	Graphics/Media
Advertising	Printing
Trade Shows	Librarian
Protocol	Historian

Qualifications

Talented people come from different backgrounds, with different experiences and educational credentials. There are no *absolutely-have-to-haves;* however, as a starting point or baseline, consider the following:

- Education: A college degree as a minimum; an advanced degree for the senior communications professionals. Related degrees might include:
  - Communications
  - Public Relations
  - Journalism
  - Business
  - Marketing
  - Psychology
  - Computer Science
  - Graphic Design
  - Videography, Cinematography
  - other related degrees, including those closely associated with the primary business of the organization
- Experience: Look for demonstrated, verifiable experience doing the same or similar work for the position being filled, such as work in:
  - media, reporting, editing
  - employee communications
  - community outreach, nonprofit and volunteer organizations
  - sales and marketing
  - business writing

- o web development
- o graphic design
- o videography, cinematography
- o other related fields and for organizations related to your industry or field
- Professional associations: Membership in professional associations is often an indication of a person's commitment to a profession or field. Among the many, some of the more prominent professional associations related to communications include:
  - o American Advertising Association (AAA)
  - o American Marketing Association
  - o Association of Marketing and Communication Professionals (AMCP)
  - o Association of Women in Communications
  - o International Association of Business Communicators (IABC)
  - o National Association of Black Journalists
  - o Public Relations Society of America (PRSA)
  - o Social Media Association
  - o Society of American Business Editors and Writers (Sigma Delta Chi Foundation)

Strive for Diversity in Staffing

The objective in striving to achieve diversity is not to placate every possible demographic group in society or make your employee profile look better, but rather to draw out and capture the best thinking and ideas to help the organization achieve its business objectives.[30] In building a Communications staff, strive for diversity in racial, ethnic, cultural, gender, sexual orientation, age and educational backgrounds to ensure representation, respect and sensitivity for differences in thought, preferences and experiences represented in your organization and industry.

Parting Thoughts on Staffing

- A place at the table—As a leader, ensure that your senior Communications staff officer serves alongside your other primary staff advisors as a peer. As discussion takes place and decisions are made, your Communications lead should be there with your Human Resources, Operations, Logistics, Legal, and Investor Relations advisors, participating in the dialogue, solving issues, and helping to shape a course of action in the best interest of the organization. In doing so, that person contributes by bringing a necessary and important Communications perspective to the leader's table.

- If for any reason you are not 100 percent confident in and comfortable with your senior Communications lead, then you might have the wrong person in the position. Get someone in there who is on the same wavelength as you. Trust is essential.

- Beyond the meetings, be accessible and make time for Communications—over a cup of coffee in the morning, in the car on the way to the airport, popping in on the way out the door: "Anything we need to talk about?" or "Any suggestions for my talk to new employees tomorrow morning?" Proximity helps. Position your Communications lead nearby—down the hall, or at least on the same floor.

- Legally speaking, understand that your Communications and Legal advisors are often at opposite ends of the communications continuum. Predictably, your Communications person will advise "maximum disclosure, minimum delay." Your Chief Counsel will advise "minimum disclosure, maximum delay." Both are doing their jobs. Depending on the circumstances, either may be right. As an example, in the event of an accident or incident, your Communications director may recommend a swift, decisive statement to head off potential negative public reaction or wild speculation about really what happened. For the same situation, your Legal advisor may recommend no statement, anticipating litigation down the road. Hear both, weigh the risks of each, and make the call!

Leader's Takeaway

An organization of any size should have a professional communicator on staff advising the boss and staff and serving the organization. Don't underestimate or sell short the impact a good Communications program can have. If your business is not large enough to justify a Communications department, identify duties and functions that are important to you and create a job description for an individual or a small right-size staff that makes sense for your organization.

CHAPTER 6

STRATEGY AND PLANNING

Strategy and planning are related, but not the same. Strategy is the big picture—the macro-view—where the organization needs to go to be successful, effective, profitable, whatever the goal. The plan—the business or operations plan—is the micro-view. It is all about the details of how you are going to achieve the strategy. It has lots of pieces and moving parts that contribute to achieving the strategy.

There are different theories for developing a strategy and plans, but it all starts with a leader's vision. Visualizing helps a leader

> "Strategy is the big picture – the macro-view; the plan is all about details of *how* – the micro-view."

crystallize and put into words what he or she wants the organization to be or achieve. It's big picture—hence, strategic. A well-articulated strategy focuses everyone's energy, effort and creative thinking on an objective. Once the leader has a clear strategy, developing an execution plan follows. It contains the nitty-gritty details—the tactics—how the strategy is going to be achieved.

It's a Logical Process

When a strategy has coalesced sufficiently in a leader's mind—your mind—where it can be shared with others, the leader presents his or her thoughts to those who make up the management team—your staff and subordinate leaders. This is done to get everyone's minds aligned. Also, their good ideas help a leader fill in gaps, refine and better articulate the strategy. The objective is to develop a strategy statement that provides clear guidance, enabling managers and departments to develop the necessary detailed plans to achieve the organization's goals. It's an important step. It's so important that many organizations do strategic development sequestered away from normal day-to-day distractions, sometimes at an off-site retreat with the intention of creating a free-thinking, no-distractions environment.

When developing a strategy, include your best people. No matter how good you think you are, involving others results in a better strategy statement and follow-on execution plans. Typically, participants are primary staff, including the senior Communicator and others with special knowledge or insights into your business or organization. Make clear to those attending that you expect active and candid participation—no turf issues or boundaries, no rubber stamping, no deferring to others to be nice. This is a time for tough self-evaluation and creative, achievable, forward-looking goal-setting. Guard against inviting too few or too many for strategy development to be productive. How many? Your call; you know your organization, and you know your good idea people. Consider no less than five others and no more than fifteen as a starting point.

By the end of your strategic development session, aim to walk away with a strategy boiled down to a couple of well-written, easy-to-understand sentences—maybe a solid paragraph.

Example of Strategic Statement

Without sacrificing sales and service to existing customers, accomplish the following goals:

- Become the federal government's preferred vendor or supplier for fasteners by providing the best quality, rapid order delivery, and a fair price.
    - o Or, increase sales by 30 percent within the next twelve months.
    - o Or, grow the organization by 25 percent by this time next year.
    - o Or, open a new office in the next town (county, state, country).
    - o Or, expand our product line or services to include …
    - o Or, improve quality and reduce rework and returns by 50 percent by …
- Efficiently use all media, platforms and opportunities to update and inform all publics—internal and external—of strategic objectives, the reasoning, intended impact, schedule, etc.
- Measure progress weekly and monthly against achievable targets by …
- Retain flexibility to adjust to market conditions and changes during …

Detailed Planning

Once a strategy is developed in sufficient detail, agreed upon, and clearly stated, it's time to present it to the organization's functional areas—the people who are going to make it happen, i.e., Manufacturing, Supply

Chain, Research and Development, Human Resources, Training, Finance, Sales and Marketing, Communications, etc.—for them to begin developing detailed plans. They must identify what they need to do or change to achieve the strategy—something they cannot do in a vacuum. Hence, they must talk with one another with an attitude of being mutually supportive. This is a team endeavor, not a competition.

An attitude of mutual support among departments translates to talking about and coordinating on a multitude of questions that need to be asked, answered and shared, such as:

- Where is the market going? What is needed? What are customers asking for?
- What is Research and Development proposing to work on?
- Does Manufacturing need to retool, reorganize?
- Can Supply Chain find sources that can meet new specification requirements?
- Can Human Resources hire new talent or retrain workers in the right numbers and skills, and by when?
- What does Finance's need to predict and budget?
- What are Sales and Marketing's concerns for the impact on existing customers, developing new business, and predicting what the competition will do?
- What are Communications' concerns for keeping employees and key publics informed, knowing schedules, updating websites, and issuing announcements and news releases?

As these questions and others are asked and addressed, the plan for achieving the strategy begins to take shape. Rarely, if ever, can a department or staff function do its part of a business plan without input and help from other departments.

When developed, functional areas (divisions, departments, branches, sections) present their detailed plans for review, revisions and ultimately approval to proceed and execute. It's not an easy process, but a good attitude focused on achieving mutual goals sure makes it less painful.

Reoccurring Theme: Diversity

Strategy and business plan development benefit from diversity of thought, and diversity comes from people with different backgrounds and experiences.[31] If you are a homogenous leadership team or organization, you are missing the good ideas, perspectives and creativity that a diverse team would give you and your organization. Take a hard look at the profile of your leadership team and organization. What's it like?

Outside Help?

Engaging a facilitator from outside your organization to moderate your strategic planning helps sometimes. One advantage is that an outsider will keep the discussion moving and on schedule. Another is that the outside facilitator does not face concerns of offending the boss or undermining a relationship among leadership staff members. When differences arise (and they will), a skillful moderator can mediate the issue or table it for the time being in the interest of making progress in other aspects of strategy development or planning.

How Far Out?

When determining strategies and plans, how far out do you look: three years, five years, ten years? A hard question to answer. It depends on many factors: how big you are now, how well established, how stable or predictable your market is, what game-changing technologies or influencers are coming down the pike, what unknowns, etc. Decisions you make today will impact where the organization will be in the future. Conservatively, it is wise to project where you would like to be in three to five years. It forces you to think bigger and broader than just next year, because then what? Projecting a few years provides a glide path, context and a progression for what you are doing today and deciding what to do tomorrow. Spend a little time thinking about where you would like to see your organization in five years, and discuss what you can do this year and next year to prepare for or move closer to that vision. Nobody can see into the future, but knowing what you know and reaching deep into experience and imagination, take an educated guess. It's all part of being a leader!

Communications in Strategy and Planning

The lead or senior Communicator should be at the table with you, your trusted staff, and your advisors throughout the planning process. If this is not the case, you may not have the right person in that position. While everyone's contribution is important, your Communications advisor is the person who will lead getting the word out and informing your publics—your employees first among them—of the organization's strategy and plans. Every leader in every department shares in the responsibility to inform employees and other publics, but it is your Communicator's primary responsibility to shape, adapt, transmit and monitor strategic and planning messaging on all available platforms. He or she is a critical player, and as a leader, you need a strong person in that position.

The Communications plan is a part of the business plan. It should be tied directly to achieving the organization's objectives.[32] Anything else is a distraction and wasted effort. What should you expect to see in the Communications plan? As a minimum, look for a plan that contains:

- Important publics: employees (maybe even further seg-mented—professional, scientific/technical, administrative, other?), investors, suppliers, customers, community, others
- Messaging consistent with your strategic objective(s) but crafted and tailored for each public based on their interest in your organization and how your strategy affects them, re-membering *one size does not fit all*
- Responses to anticipated questions and potential objections
- Development and distribution of talking points for other lead-ers in your organization, ensuring everyone is speaking with one voice
- A rollout schedule for announcements, website updates, and news releases
- Production of a new videos, briefing slides, supporting litera-ture (posters, brochures, etc.), and collateral materials
- New or updated advertising
- Special efforts, such as making leaders available for interviews and speaking opportunities
- Feedback mechanisms to measure and gauge effectiveness of how well the message is getting out and being received
- A schedule to reassess and adjust the Communications plan based on feedback
- Budget to support plan execution

Parting Thoughts

Two parting thoughts: Developing a strategy and plans are the road map to achieving business goals. Communications is an important piece of both. First, creating a strategy and developing plans must be undertaken with diligence and executed with enthusiasm. Second, assuming you invested a lot of time and effort into developing your strategy and plans, keep them close at hand, review them frequently, talk about them, and don't be timid about making updates as circumstances change. These are living documents meant to evolve.

Leader's Takeaway

- Strategy planning starts in your head. Knowing what you know, ask yourself these questions: Where does your organization need to go from here, and how is it going to get there?
- Once you can answer these questions, assemble your trusted staff, share your thoughts, and solicit their ideas to formulate a good strategic statement.
- Then, share your strategic vision with leaders at all levels and commence detailed planning.
- Communications will have an especially important role in getting the word out and everyone on board.
- It's not easy, but when done well, diligent strategy development and planning get everyone working together to achieve common goals.

CHAPTER 7

INTERNAL: EMPLOYEE COMMUNICATIONS

Generally, the more members of a leader's team know about the organization, what's going on, and why it's important, the more supportive and better performing they are.[33] And the more they know what's on a leader's mind and what his or her expectations are, the better able they are to deliver what the leader wants. It's your job as the leader to create an environment in which employees are well-informed, understand their roles, and know what the endgame is.

> "Employees are perhaps a leader's most important public and often overlooked."

Take every opportunity from new employee orientations to periodic "all hands" updates to informal drop-ins to stay connected with your members of your organization and keep them well-informed. And when you cannot be there in person, get help from Communications to use other means to provide a steady flow of up-to-date and relevant information. The more you do to keep your team well-informed, the better your organization will perform and the better morale will be. If it's not obvious, performance and morale are related. High-performing outfits tend to have better morale.

At the same time, not everybody needs to know everything. Between you and your staff—Communications, Human Resources, others—decide how much information they need and how deep to go. Determine what is appropriate and useful for subordinates and employees to know. Clearly, there are very good reasons to limit or protect certain information.

Throughout this discussion of communications, emphasis is placed on the audience's perspective as the listener—receiver of the message. This is especially important for employees—perhaps a leader's most important public and often overlooked or neglected because the leader is focused on existing and prospective customers or solving problems that pop up every day. Make time for employees!

As you communicate with employees, conveying necessary information and guidance, understand that most employees want to do a good job for their own personal satisfaction as well as for the collective good of the organization. Most recognize that when the organization succeeds, they succeed. But also understand that much of what you convey to subordinates is filtered through their concerns about job security, chances for advancement, and other questions, such as:

- Why am I doing this? Is it a necessary function?
- Does anyone notice or appreciate what I do?
- What does my supervisor think of me and my performance?

The steady flow of positive and encouraging information goes a long way toward allaying anxieties and freeing employees to concentrate on doing their jobs.

Principles and Process

When communicating with employees, repetition, multiple channels and feedback are especially important elements in the process.

- **Repetition:** Many people need to be told something more than once before it sticks. Think of being told, "Don't leave your wet towel on the bathroom floor." How many times do you have to hear this before you hang it up? Also, more than likely, not everyone was present when you said it the last time, or the last three times. Finally, to some people, it's not important or it doesn't sink in until you say it over and over. Whatever the reason, although it is annoying to some, repetition is necessary for the word to get through.

- **Multiple channels:** Use different channels to communicate with internal publics: in-person conversations, speaking to small groups, briefings and updates to larger groups, the boss's blog, email, articles on your organization's intranet and internal publications, videos, video conferencing ... whatever you have. Everyone is different as to how, where and when they get their information. Habits and preferences vary: watching the television while dressing, with a first cup of coffee, going online, reading a newspaper, listening to the radio while driving, talking with family, friends or coworkers, or any combination of these. Learning what's important at work is very much the same. Use all channels available to you to extend your reach.

- **Feedback:** Feedback is another important part of the communication process. It's the other end of the two-way process. In organizations, information should flow from the top down *and* from the bottom up. The latter isn't always as robust as the former. Ensure that there are provisions and channels for information to flow back up the management chain. Feedback tells you if your message got through or not, and if it was understood as you intended. It will also give you indications of interest and morale, and it will open the door to information, intelligence and issues you may not have been expecting. Maintain an open mind as feedback flows. A few cautions:

- o Don't shoot the messenger if the feedback is not good or what you expected.
- o Don't turn a deaf ear to things you don't want to hear. If there is negative feedback, better that you learn about it sooner than later, and address it. Remember, leaders are problem solvers.
- o Don't allow gatekeepers—intermediate managers and administrative staff—to cut off, edit out, or delete negative feedback in attempts to protect you or protect themselves from something they should have handled.

Have a Program

Having a formal program forces leaders to keep members of the organization focused and updated. If it's on the master calendar, more than likely it's going to happen. Keeping workers informed is time well spent, not extra or a chore. Your entire leadership team should contribute and participate, but you are the driver. What's important to you—the leader, the boss—magically becomes important to everyone who works for you! What's in a good Employee Communications program?

- **A good new employee orientation:** Getting new employees off to a good start both in attitude and responsibilities begins here. A good orientation can reduce the learning curve, impacting productivity by weeks. Let it be known to Human Resources and the rest of your staff that you consider these orientations to be very important and that you expect their cooperation and participation to make new employee orientations as good as they can be. As a leader, you should personally participate, addressing these new employees. Typically, your comments include:
  - o A sincere welcome: "Glad to have you on our team; we need your best effort."
  - o The organization's mission, goals, reason to be
  - o The importance of every person contributing in different ways
  - o A brief statement of the market environment and how the organization fits in
  - o The importance and expectation of compliance with policy, procedures and ethical standards
  - o The need to work as a team, supporting and respecting one another
  - o Where to go or whom to go to for questions, problems, ethical dilemmas and uncomfortable situations, such as sexual harassment
  - o Other topics you deem to be important, timely and relevant
- **Recognition:** Just as important as attending new employee orientations when you can is attending promotions, awards ceremonies and retirements. Your attendance not only recognizes those being honored but also communicates your

genuine interest in and appreciation for what all employees contribute.

- **Periodic "all hands" updates:** In addition to your regular staff meetings, hold periodic (quarterly, semiannual, annual) updates for all employees whom you are responsible for leading or directing. Employees need to see you from time-to-time and hear the unvarnished situation—the good and not-so-good news. Other members of your staff can and should participate, covering such things as financials, policy and procedure changes, pay and benefits—whatever you and your staff determine employees need to know. Aim to keep these updates a reasonable length—perhaps an hour, including a time for questions and answers. What should *you* cover in periodic updates for employees?
  - The business environment
  - Challenges, obstacles, big projects and initiatives, new business, lost business
  - How the organization is doing by whatever metrics are relevant, what's going well, and what isn't
  - Who the competition is and what they are doing
  - Guidance, direction, and what needs to change
  - Recognition of outstanding individual and team efforts
  - Other topics you deem appropriate—administrative, policy, announcements, etc.
- **Team meetings at all levels:** Insist that managers and supervisors at all levels hold regular meetings to keep subordinates informed. These can be daily, weekly, monthly—whatever makes sense for the work at hand. These meeting are important because they give intermediate leaders the opportunity to relay

information, convert general guidance to specific instructions, and cover job-related details. Also, regular meetings reinforce the role and stature of supervisors as the source of information and direction for employees. To many employees, their immediate supervisor is the face of organization and the biggest influence affecting their job satisfaction and morale.

- **Coach and mentor:** Senior leaders have an added responsibility to help intermediate and junior leaders grow and succeed. Senior leaders influence junior leaders by their example, but also by providing regular guidance and feedback, creating opportunities, and relaying relevant and timely information that they can adapt and translate to specific taskings for their teams.

- **A content rich and user friendly resource for employees:** Maintain a robust organizational intranet with up-to-date and useful information. It should be a place that is user friendly where employees regularly go for an array of information about projects, milestones, taskings, events, policies, procedures, checklists, Human Resources and Finance forms, benefits—whatever is useful and helpful. In many organizations, Information Technology creates the intranet's architecture and Communications has overall responsibility for management, formatting, and organization of the intranet. Departments and staff sections (Human Resources, Legal, Finance, Security, Safety, etc.) are responsible for their content. What's important is that responsibilities for managing and maintaining the intranet are clearly defined. For organizations in which not all employees work at desks and have individual computers, provide kiosks, libraries or help desks—alternatives—where employees can access the information they need.

- **Emergency notification system:** Ensure your organization has a primary and backup rapid notification system in place for emergencies and events, either human-, facility- or nature-related.[34] It might include computer notification, personal cell phones, a public address system, alarms, messengers, and even a duress code. The system should be explained during new employee orientations, reviewed periodically, and exercised/practiced from time-to-time.

  o A human-caused event could be a medical emergency, a disgruntled former or current employee with a firearm, a domestic dispute that follows one or the other from home to work, unpredictable behavior by a mentally disturbed person, a physical altercation (a fight) between employees, or a random incident.

  o A facility-related emergency might be a fire, a water main break, a power outage, a heating, ventilation, or air conditioning failure, a laboratory accident, chemical or radiation contamination, a leak, or an explosion.

  o A natural event could be a tornado, hurricane, flood, thunder and lightning storm, blizzard, or ice storm.

No one has a crystal ball to see what emergency might occur in the future. But if plans are in place for likely events for the type of organization you are or the region where you are located, they can be easily and quickly adapted for a similar event. There will be plenty of decisions a leader will have to make on the fly when an emergency occurs, but having a plan is a good starting point for taking control of the situation. Make sure there are plans in place and instructions are clear: "Shelter in place," "Evacuate the building immediately," "Danger—shooter (or fire) in building A—move to buildings B and

C," "Immediately move away from windows," and so on. Contingency planning for bad things happening is a leader's responsibility.

Seize Informal Opportunities to Connect

Create opportunities to connect with and interact with employees in less formal ways. Some may be scheduled, but many can occur during your normal routine. Here are some suggestions. If they resemble opportunities you can adapt and do, great. If not, they will get you thinking of ways you can connect with rank-and-file workers in your organization.

- When you arrive at work, greet the security guard, receptionist, and others you encounter on the way in or in the elevator. "Quiet night? Anything unusual? Do we have a lot of visitors today? Cold out there!" Say something to people you meet on the way into the office. It's banter that opens the door for an exchange however brief. Same for on the way out at day's end.

- Go to the cafeteria or snack bar and through the line, like everyone else. Talk to the person in front of or behind you. Talk with the servers, the cashiers. Again, brief exchanges: "Haven't seen you here before. What do you do? Didn't your son just graduate? How's he doing?" If you are a very busy leader, try to make it to the cafeteria once or twice a week. Look for opportunities to start a conversation. Ask open-ended questions to get the other person talking, not questions that can be answered with a one-word *yes* or *no*. Resist eating at your desk or having meals and coffee brought to you all the time.

- Segment and meet with groups of employees from time-to-time. Have Human Resources select and invite five to fifteen people who are relatively new or young, mid-career, or senior (or any other groupings) in your organization to have light breakfast with you, or lunch, or pizza, or a cheese-and-veggie platter at the end of the workday. The purpose of these group meetings is to hear their observations, concerns and suggestions. To get the discussion going, you need talk briefly about what you hope to take away, i.e., to listen and hear what's on their minds. Resist being judgmental or defensive or launching into lengthy explanations about *why this* or *that*. So long as you don't hijack the session, meetings with smaller groups also give you an opportunity to coach or provide career advice appropriate for the group.

- Walk around, as in "management by walking around."[35] Every once in a while, walk through your workplace—the cube farms, shops, labs, where the work is done—places you rarely or never go, and stop and chat. Introduce yourself, and ask: "What are you doing? Is there a better way?" You'll learn a lot. And, for many, it's a big deal when the boss talks with an employee, shows interest in what a person is doing, and asks for an opinion. Go solo—dismiss the strap-hangers and note-takers. Of course, this makes intermediate managers and supervisors nervous. That's okay. Back-brief them later.

- If your organization has multiple sites or offices, use your visits to these other locations for more than the primary reason you are there in the first place—meeting, updates or problem-solving.[36] Not always, but from time-to-time, use the downtime or mealtime to connect with workers in ways described above. As a minimum, do a walk-through of the facility so employees see you. They need to see you in the flesh. Even something as a simple as a leader's walk-through is significant for some—perhaps dinner table conversation at home that night.

- Have a "hip pocket talk" handy. It is a standard presentation that you've thought about, planned and can give at a moment's notice. It contains key points that are important to you, are recurring themes or issues, and can easily be geared in their level of detail and length to any audience and circumstance. As a leader, don't pass up an opportunity to address and say something meaningful, especially to employees.

Other Ways and Means

- Boss's blog: Write a couple of paragraphs once a week about what's on your mind or what's especially important. Let it be informal in tone. Let your personality come through. If you are too busy, have someone in Communications ghost-write a first draft with your guidance. Then edit it to make it your own.
- Use technology. Place televisions and electronic crawl lines in lobbies, break rooms, cafeteria. Good for brief announcements: "Red Cross blood drive today," "United Way," "Welcome," "Happy Thanksgiving," "Schools open tomorrow—drive carefully," "Reminder—benefit options due Friday," and so on.
- Signage at entrances and gates to parking lots—same as above.
- Bulletin boards: Have a bulletin board on your intranet and televisions, as well as old-fashioned cork boards near entrances and in the cafeteria and break rooms. Divide it for official

organizational notices and unofficial announcements, such as "House, car, boat, snow tires for sale," "Bake sale for …," "Company softball game tomorrow at 5:00 p.m.," "Kittens need a home," and "Volunteers needed for …" Bulletin boards provide an alternative to unsightly and out-of-control flyers going up in stairwells, restrooms and elevators. Important: bulletin boards must be managed for neatness, kept up-to-date, and monitored for appropriateness—a Communications function.

Leader's Takeaway

- "If I do all you are suggesting, I will never have time to do my job," you may be thinking.
    - Number one: Keeping the people who work in your organization well informed *is* doing your job.
    - Number two: If you do it right and with help from your staff, many of the ideas suggested here will become part of your daily rhythm and you won't even notice it. You will have the satisfaction of knowing you are using your time well and building a well-informed and more cohesive organization.
- Be seen and create opportunities to connect with the people who do the work. They need to see and hear you from time to time.
- Make sure plans are in place for emergency situations, both for the safety and well-being of those for whom you are responsible and for business continuity.

CHAPTER 8

EXTERNAL: MEDIA RELATIONS

We're all part of a larger universe. To survive and thrive, we must interact with those outside our immediate circle. In organizations and businesses, communicating externally is largely accomplished through the media—hence, media relations. We used to say press relations, but that's now dated. *Media relations* is a collective term for an organization's interaction with newspapers, television, radio, trade publications, websites, social media, blogs—in other words, all communications channels, traditional and newer electronic channels—communicating with the public at large and selected publics.

Many leaders are ambivalent about the media, principally because it is out of their control and has a large potential for damage. In recent years, confidence has diminished in media's objectivity and fairness—unfortunate, but understandable in these times. In theory and at its best, the media performs an important function in a democracy. Because citizens do not have the time, resources, background and sometimes interest to monitor what government, industry and other institutions are doing that affect us in positive and negative ways, the media serves as the *watchdog* on our behalf, reporting on, educating us about, and alerting us to what we need to know to be informed and participating citizens. Don't lose faith. Most people working in the media understand their role and responsibility, take it seriously, and know that we depend on them.

Approaching media relations positively, proactively and skillfully when working with the media can be a tremendous asset and boost helping leaders and organizations achieve their business objectives. It is an area in which a leader can benefit by knowing how the media functions and having a Communications professional on staff who knows the ropes. Some of what is covered here may be new to you; however, most of it, if not all and more, is the bread and butter of what Communications professionals on your staff know, routinely do, and should be advising. The purpose here is making you aware of how the media operates. As situations arise, between what is addressed here and the counsel your Communications staff provides, you'll be better prepared to recognize the potential advantages and traps when working with the media.

Having good relationships with the media is important in good times and bad. It starts with your Communications (or Media Relations) lead and you cultivating a rapport with reporters, editors and news directors in your area and field. Their business is reporting the news. They are going to do it *with* or *without* your help. It's better for everyone if you are involved. Over time, if you are a good source of interesting and relevant news, then your relationship will likely be a win-win situation for both you and the media outlets with whom you work. On the other hand, if the news you offer is shallow and patently self-promoting, or if your first contact occurs when the media comes asking questions about a bad news situation, then the relationship is likely to be uncomfortable, difficult, or adversarial.

Members of the media are approachable. Get to know them. Introduce yourself. Visit them in their offices or at a trade show, or invite them to your facility for a "show and tell." The more they know about your organization or what you do, the better able they will be to understand your perspective and report it accurately. Take the initiative. Make an effort to understand their editorial focus, how they operate, who the players are, and who their audience is.

Learn the Rules of the Game

When you meet reporters, editors and news directors, one of the first things you want to accomplish is a clear and mutual understanding of the rules of attribution. They are the rules of the game in dealing with the media. When you interact with the media representatives, know what it means to be talking in the following ways:

- *On the record*—Whatever is said in conversation or in an interview is useable and attributable in a story to the person who said it. If it is not clearly specified beforehand, assume any comments made with a representative of any news organization is on the record.
- *Not for attribution*—Whatever is told to a reporter is useable in a story but is not attributable to a specific person. Example: "A source familiar with the situation said …"
- *For background only*—A variation of *not for attribution*. Sometimes, it is necessary to fill in or educate a reporter on background information to provide context or significance. In this case, a reporter can use the information as if it is in the public domain, historical, a matter widely known and accepted.

- *Off the record—Off the record* is an agreement between a source and a reporter not to use information provided or found out at all. It can be useful where matters of security, privacy or propriety are at stake. However, discussing matters off the record is risky and requires a high level of trust, usually gained over time.

Trust

Since the word has come up, trust is an important element in media relations. A reporter should expect that the information you, a source, provide is the truth. Likewise, you, the source, have a right to expect and trust that the information you provide—facts and context—is reported accurately. You are both professionals with a job to do and should respect the position and perspective each has. Deliberately providing or reporting false information or misinformation is unethical and will undermine any credibility or relationship between all parties. This is easy to accept and agree to in theory but is sometimes harder to put into practice when stakes are high, issues are controversial, passions are strong, or reputations hang in the balance. More on this later.

Related to trust, sometimes you are asked a question that you cannot answer for legitimate reasons. If this happens, tell the reporter *why*. It may be a matter of privacy, security, policy, or competitive intelligence, such as a trade secret or research findings. The real pros, the experienced ones, the reporters for whom you are a regular source and with whom you have a rapport, are willing to listen to your reason and reach an acceptable accommodation or work-around.

Single Point of Contact

Have a single point of contact in your organization for communicating with the media. Whether it is a person by name or an office, make sure the official source for queries and access to your organization is known to the media. Likewise, it should be a matter of policy made clear to everyone within your organization that all contact with members of the media be initiated by or directed to this single person or office—your Communications director, Media Relations manager, or Communications office. This ensures that management knows of the media's interest and that the flow of information is in the right hands. Having a single point of contact doesn't mean that only one person speaks with the media. When appropriate, the Communications or Media Relations manager will coordinate for others in the organization, based on their position, authority or expertise, to answer questions or be interviewed.

The policy of having a single point—person or office—to communicate with the media requires emphasis and repeating in these times when anyone with a cell phone is a potential news source. Also, as relationships are established with media representatives, request their cooperation to communicate with your designated media contact as the authorized and official source for information in your organization.

Equal Treatment

The media industry is competitive. Media organizations compete with one another to be first in reporting the news and best at telling the story. Your part is to treat all media the same, giving them a level playing field in the competition of reporting your news. When your organization has news to report, the same information should be provided to all media organizations that have an interest in your organization and at the same time to the extent possible. For larger organizations, this is usually accomplished by issuing a news release over a wire service, such as PRNewswire or Business Wire, and simultaneously posting it on your organization's website. Some media will use it, and others won't. From those that do, you can expect a phone call asking for more information, clarification or amplification.

If you are a small organization or do not subscribe to a wire service, maintain a list of media that have an interest in and have reported on your organization in the past. Endeavor to get your news to them all as close to the same time as possible.

If your organization has a major announcement or news, such as opening a new facility, acquiring another company, or winning an especially large contract, holding a news briefing (also called a press conference) may be appropriate. A news briefing ensures that all interested media outlets get the news at the same time and have an opportunity to ask questions. Communication and Media professionals know the steps and logistics for planning and hosting news briefings.

Exclusivity

Because of the competitive nature of the news industry, media organizations are looking for a fresh or different angle on the news to distinguish them from their competitors, all of whom have the same news release. When you issue a news release, you can expect calls from reporters asking for more. They are probing for a detail or nugget of information that no one else has. You should anticipate this and be ready to respond or to say you have nothing further to add.

Not every detail is included in news releases. Knowing this, answer questions to the extent that you can and are authorized to re-spond. However, do not volunteer additional information that another reporter from a different news organization has asked about. That reporter's experience, knowledge and initiative in asking good ques-tions are his or her competitive advantage and should be respected. If challenged, "Why didn't you tell all of us these additional facts?" your response is, "Everyone got the same news release. They called and asked specific questions; you didn't."

Editorial Focus

Know something of the editorial focus of the publications and other media you are targeting. Match and address your news to appropriate publications, editors and departments, i.e. "Attention: Business Editor" (or Innovation Section, People in the News, Executive Changes, New Products and Services, etc.). If the news is a good fit for the media outlet and its target audience, it will get published or used. It's the job of your Communications staff to know which media are likely to be receptive to your news and which are not, and to package and direct it accordingly.

News Value Changes

The value of news changes. Timing matters. A major event, good or bad, will likely dominate the news and take up all available print space and broadcast time. Your news, although significant and newsworthy in your mind, will likely slip down on the scale of importance when competing with the major event. On the other hand, an event over which you have no control might catapult your organization into the news for good or bad reasons. Say you produce bottled water. Then a hurricane hits your region. Suddenly, your organization goes from producing a ho-hum commodity to being an important supplier of a critical necessity. Still, on another day—a slow news day—a news release your organization distributed that wasn't used (perhaps in an editor's view, was considered marginal in news value) may get plugged in a week or two later. The nature of what constitutes news is fickle and sometimes unpredictable, depending on what else is happening.

QUESTION: WHAT IS NEWS?
ANSWER: …WHAT IS NEW, SIGNIFICANT, INTERESTING, UNUSUAL

IN GENERAL	IN BUSINESS
Conflict, war, crime	New product feature, service, capability
Government, politics	Award, contract, opportunity
Scandals, sex	New facility expansion, relocation
Human interest, underdog, victim	Merger, acquisition
Money, economy	Significant accomplishment, discovery, development, research, milestone
Unusual, quirky	
Celebrity, entertainment, sports	Impacting jobs - hiring, layoff, strike
Affecting people - health, science, environment, weather progress, jobs, closeness	Donation, sponsorship
	New top executive

"Dog bites man" is not news; but "man bites dog" is news.

The Venerable News Release

From a business perspective, most stories, whether they end up being print, broadcast or digital, begin with the venerable news release. Although drafting and issuing a news release is the most visible duty of your Communications/Media manager or department, it is just one tool and one function of the job. See chapter 5, "Staffing," for a more complete discussion of media duties and responsibilities. But here are a few things you, as a leader, can look for as news releases cross your desk for your review and approval.

- Every news release should answer the questions of *who, what, where, when, why,* and *how.* These are known in journalism as the five Ws and H.[37]
- The headline on the news release is a *working headline* telling a reporter what the news release is about in a few words. It should be brief and descriptive. The headline you see or hear when the story is published will be different, usually written by an editor and not by the reporter who wrote the story.
- The first paragraph of a news release is the *summary lead,* meaning just that—a summary of the news. And it should be brief—preferably one sentence, but not more than three. A well-written summary lead will answer the five Ws and H questions. Subsequent paragraphs provide the details.
- News releases are written in the format or shape of an *inverted pyramid,* meaning that after the summary lead, paragraphs will address the most important information first. Other details will be addressed in descending order of importance, paragraph by paragraph. Editors and news directors *edit to fit* the space or time they have or want to allocate to a given story. If a news release is well-written in journalistic style, i.e. an inverted pyramid, an editor will cut paragraphs from the bottom, knowing that the more important elements of the story are in the top. Admittedly, this sometimes results in a choppy story, but it's efficient.
- Well-written news releases stand a good chance of being published as written by your Communications staff. Media outlets—newspapers, television and radio stations, magazines

and websites—have small staffs and often do not have the luxury or time to rewrite the news. Another reason for distributing well-written pieces is that the more a news release is edited or rewritten, the greater the chance an error could be introduced or a change in nuance, tone or context might occur. The person who drafts your news releases should be an excellent writer who knows journalistic standards and has a good understanding of your organization.

- Quotations give life to a news release compared to a third-person narrative, making an otherwise boring piece more interesting. When appropriate, include a quote from a recognized person in authority or a subject matter expert telling the news or stating its significance. As a practical matter, a leader or expert will often allow or request the writer to draft a quotation on his or her behalf, subject to review. This gives the writer license to create a quote that fits the context of the news release and adds significant information. Also, it expedites the drafting process. During the review and approval process, the person to whom the quote is attributed can accept it as written, edit or modify the quote, or create his or her own quote. Nothing should go forward without complete buy-in by the person to whom the quote is attributed.

- A photo, illustration, chart or map accompanying a news release enhances the attractiveness and likelihood of the release in the eyes of editors because it adds a visual element to the story, providing options for layout and design. Also, words and pictures working together tell a story better. Whatever visual is provided needs to be high quality for reproduction purposes and contributes to advancing the story.

- Have a streamlined approval process for news releases in your organization. The process should move quickly. Have a deadline for a response—minutes or no more than a few hours, not days. Anticipate news events and have news releases drafted, circulated and approved in advance. If review of a news release gets lost in inboxes, it stands the chance of becoming stale, and stale news loses its value—*it's news that isn't new.* Request comments, not for people to edit or rewrite the release. The writing and rewriting are the responsibility of the Communications staff, and pieces written by committee are usually not done well. Not everyone needs to see every news release in advance, but make sure other leaders in your organization see it to ensure they are informed and can speak about it if asked. Sometimes it helps to anticipate likely questions and have approved responses ready to go.
- News releases should be kept reasonable in length—a double-spaced page or two, maybe a bit more. Not every detail needs to be included. All news releases list a media contact in your organization. If the news is of interest or in a news organization's sweet spot, you can expect a call from an editor, reporter, or news director with questions or requesting more information.
- A good way to ensure a news release *doesn't* get published or aired is to offer a blatantly self-promoting piece or a piece that has little or no news value. Not only will this release not see the light of day, but also it will hurt your reputation as a news source and diminish chances of future news releases being favorably considered.
- Control of your news release ends when you distribute it. An editor is not bound to use it, can edit it, may use some or all of

it, may use it as a basis for an interview, or may add information to it from other sources. This is why a well-conceived and well-written news release is so important. It should answer the obvious questions. Loss of control once a news release has been issued can be unsettling, but it's how the game is played.

**JOURNALISM'S INVERTED PYRAMID
FOR REPORTING THE NEWS**

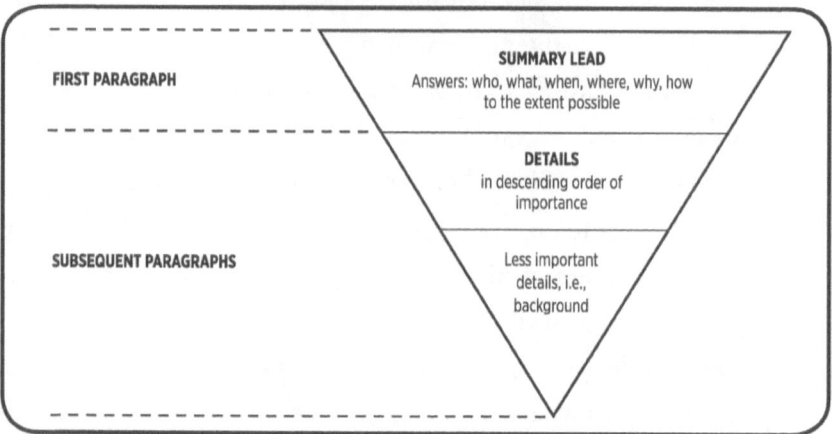

The Art of the Interview

Since you are a leader, reporters from the media will likely request to interview you from time-to-time. Doing interviews comes with the territory. Look at it as an opportunity to get information out about you, your organization, and your product or service. Assuming the resulting piece is favorable, the article or video segment is free advertising. It beats paying for an expensive ad or promotional piece, and because it is editorial, there is the presumption that editors have reviewed the interview and determined it to have interest and value compared to the *I-can-say-(almost)-anything-I-want* in a paid-for ad.

On the other side of the coin, interviews have risks and traps that you should be aware of. An experienced Communications or Media manager will help you recognize these hazards and coach you on ways to handle them. Many leaders are comfortable doing interviews. For others, the prospect of having to do an interview is terrifying. It doesn't have to be—if you're prepared.

In approaching interviews, have your own agenda. Decide what you want to gain from doing the interview. Most organizations, large and small, have a business plan with goals and objectives. Even though interviews are often externally initiated by a reporter or media outlet, they represent opportunities for an organization to further achieve its objectives. Use the interview as a stepping stone to tell your story. This takes thinking and planning by you and your Communications lead. Figure out how one or more of your objectives can be integrated into your responses. Go into the interview with your own agenda—what you want to get out of it—not just to answer questions.

Consider a *before, during* and *after* approach to understand the dynamics of the interview, get the most out of it, and stay out of trouble.

Before

- All interviews should be coordinated through your Communications or Media manager. If you or anyone in your organization is contacted by a reporter, he or she should be referred to the right person on your Communications staff so that the decision to do the interview can be properly vetted.

- Make sure leadership within your organization knows about the interview and concurs.
- Who should do the interview? Rule of thumb: it should be the person best able to answer the questions and represent the organization on the subject at hand.
  - If a reporter from *The New York Times, CNN* or CBS's *60 Minutes* calls, or if the scope of the interview is wide ranging, the organization's CEO or president would likely be the best person to do the interview. A senior executive is in a better position to provide the big picture and context. Also, some companies use interviews with top executives to position or reinforce authority or status. On the other hand, if financials are the topic, then the CFO is probably the right person to do the interview. In other situations, it could be a program manager, senior scientist, or subject matter expert—*the person most knowledgeable.*
  - But it's not *just* knowledge. Other factors affect who speaks for the organization. People who are likeable, articulate, poised, and able to make technical, scientific or complicated matters understood are good candidates. Likewise, a person who is long-winded, too technical or too narrow in focus, or disheveled may not be.
  - One-person interviews are preferred for clarity and continuity, but it may be necessary to team a big-picture or high-level person with a technical or scientific person to effectively answer the questions and tell the story. Thought and objectivity need to go into deciding who is best to do an interview.

- Prepare: If you expect a good outcome from an interview, prepare for it. Don't do an interview cold or on the fly. Since you're the expert being interviewed, you should know what's going to be discussed. It's perfectly acceptable to ask the reporter what he or she wants to talk about. Some reporters will even give you the questions. If the reporter balks, tell him or her that knowing the questions, or at least the topics, will help you provide more substantive responses. Between what the reporter tells you he or she wants to talk about and your knowledge of the subject, you and your Communications or Media manager should be able to figure out how the interview will go and help you achieve your objectives.

- Research: Make sure you have the best available information for likely questions. Sometimes a "prep" meeting with or information papers by subject matter experts are helpful. It's okay to go into an interview with notes on key points you want to make.

- Track record: Know something about the reporter and media outlet you are about to meet. Your Communications staff should know and provide this background information. Review what they have reported in the past. This will give you an indication of their level of knowledge about your field and organization, and if they have an editorial bias or slant.

- Sometimes reporters—especially general or inexperienced reporters—don't know what to ask. They may not have detailed knowledge of your organization or have done their homework preparing to interview you. This presents an opportunity for your Communications lead to influence the direction of the interview. A preliminary conversation between a member of your Communications staff and the reporter is an opportunity to discuss what is hot or relevant or what priorities or challenges your organization is facing, and it may result in actual questions or at least an outline for the interview. Some reporters appreciate this approach and are amenable to suggestions; others are not. On the other hand, some reporters are specialists and will surprise you with the depth of their knowledge of your industry and organization. Know with whom you are speaking!

- Anticipate and prepare for hard questions. Spend some time predicting difficult, hard, hostile, potential-bad-news, and inappropriate questions. Craft fact-based responses ahead of time. Know how far you want to go in answering difficult questions so as not to violate privacy, security or propriety information restrictions, or get into an argument with a reporter.

- Set parameters for the interview. Determine and agree on where the interview will take place and for how long, and stick to it. These details are the responsibility of your Communications staff to coordinate. Do not allow interruptions during the interview or take calls, and leave your cell phone in the desk and out of view. Give the interview your full attention.

- Location: Conference rooms are good places for interviews. If you have a nice office with comfortable chairs or a conference table, use them. Do not sit behind your desk with a reporter on the other side. Having something in between unnecessarily separates you and reporter and can create a "we-them" dynamic. Wherever you do the interview, sit up straight or lean forward. Your body language speaks to your interest level.

When being videotaped or interviewed on live television, do it standing, not sitting. You'll look better.

During

- Know the rules for attribution: *on the record, not for attribution, for background only, off the record*, as discussed earlier.
- Consider everything to be on the record. When doing an interview, from the moment the reporter arrives to when the reporter walks out the door, everything is on the record. Do not say anything you would regret seeing in print or hearing again before or after you sit down to do the interview.
- Be polite, friendly and professional. Remember, this is business. Trying to be clever, witty or charming can be a distraction and may not create the professional business atmosphere that an interview should have. Play it straight.
- Have another person present. Insist that your Communications lead or Media manager be present and record the interview. Many reporters record interviews also. Recording conversations requires the knowledge and concurrence of all parties involved. There should be no objections. Recording creates a record for reference and accuracy.[38] However, sometimes recording a conversation unnerves a person and alters the tone of the interview. If you are not recording, then have a note-taker present. Also, having a Communications person present helps keep the conversation on track and prevents it from drifting outside agreed-upon parameters.
- Be concise and clear. Know what you want to say, and say it clearly and concisely. Do not drone on. Answer the question

and move on to the next one. Do not volunteer or add peripheral information. Long-winded and complicated responses increase the chances for misunderstanding or of a reporter missing the important point.

- Avoid jargon and technical language. Every profession has its terminology, abbreviations, acronyms, and expressions that are clear to members of the profession—insiders—but are meaningless or confusing to outsiders. To the extent that you can, don't use jargon and technical language.[39] When jargon is unavoidable, define or explain terms. Do your best to talk in layman's terms without talking down to the reporter.

- Stay in your lane. During the interview, talk only about your area of responsibility or expertise, or matters that you are authorized to talk about. Avoid allowing the conversation to drift into other areas. In other words, stay in your lane. Example: "Interesting question, but I can't really say. I'd love for you to speak with our Human Resources director about that."[40]

- Don't speculate. Guessing or predicting a course of action is risky. Every situation is different. Don't get trapped into saying what you would do in a hypothetical or future situation that hasn't happened. Respond along the lines: "You're asking me to speculate. I don't like doing that. Every situation is different. When we know the facts of a specific situation, then we'll decide on a proper course of action." Also, don't guess and risk giving incorrect information.

- Deflect irrelevant or dumb questions. Reporters don't ask irrelevant or dumb questions on purpose, but it happens sometimes, usually from their not knowing your business or from inexperience. Help them out by rephrasing or redirecting the question, and then provide a response. Some examples:

- o "That's very interesting, but the real question is …"
- o "I'm not sure about that, but I will tell you what I think is important."
- o "Let me think about that. In the meantime, let me say …"

- Curve Ball: If the reporter throws you a curve ball and asks a question that you weren't expecting, it's okay to say,
  - o "Interesting question—let me think about that for a minute."
  - o "Let's come back to this question later, after I've had a chance to think about it."
  - o "Fair question—I'll have to call you back about that one later after I've had a chance to research it or talk with my expert on …"[41]

- Hostile reporters or questions: First and foremost, keep your cool. Do not let a reporter get under your skin or let a leading question unnerve you. Stick with the facts. You can politely but firmly disagree with how the reporter poses a question or the premise of the question. Do not let a reporter get away with asking a leading question or suggest what your response should be. In bad news situations, accept the facts, take responsibility for what is yours, and talk about what you are doing to correct, rectify or mitigate the situation. More on this later—chapter 13.

- Mistakes—If you make a mistake, mis-state, or say something that doesn't come out or sound right, correct yourself on the spot, saying something along the lines:
  - o "I mistakenly said …, but I meant to say …"

    ○ "That didn't come out like I meant it. Let me try again by saying ..."

- In wrapping up an interview, a good reporter will usually end with an open-ended question—something along these lines: "Well, thank you. You've answered all my questions. Is there anything else you would like to add?" If there is, state it: "I thought you were going to ask me about ..." or "Let me tell you what I think is very important about what we've been talking about." If not, use this as an opportunity to restate your most important point: "I just want to emphasize ..."

- Don't ask to review or approve. Don't ask to review or approve a reporter's story or video report. It's not done, and editors won't allow it. They see such a request as interference with their editorial prerogative. Your opportunity is the interview itself. Do a good job, and trust the reporter to do his or her job.

- Invite a call back. On the way out, encourage the reporter to call back if he or she needs to clarify or verify facts or information when writing or putting the story together. Sometimes memory, notes and context become fuzzy hours later. This is why recording interviews is helpful. Accuracy is in everyone's best interest.

After

- Do a critique. Before other matters take over, and while the interview is still fresh in your mind, do a quick critique on how the interview went. Invite candid observations. "You did a terrific job, boss" does nothing to help you do better on your next interview. There is always something you could have said or done better. Be tough on yourself, and expect candor from your Communications staff.

- Deliver promised information. If you owe information (charts, statistics, photos, historical facts, etc.) to the reporter, make sure you or your Communications staff provides it promptly. If you discovered that you made a mistake or provided incorrect information, you or your Communications staff should contact the reporter and clarify or correct the mistake.

- Reacting to errors: Errors, small and large, should be addressed. A basic principle of good journalism is accuracy. If minor errors are in the published or broadcasted piece, your Communications staff should call the reporter, thank him or her for the piece, and then tactfully point out the mistake. Understand that there is a difference between errors in fact and editorial slant or perspective. An error in fact is clear; however, a disagreement on editorial slant or perspective is not clear and a matter of opinion.

- If there are major errors in fact or a misrepresentation of what took place during the interview, your Communications lead should contact the reporter's editor or news director with the complaint. Having a recording helps. Expect the editor or news director to check into the matter and talk with the reporter. If after review of both sides, the editor agrees a wrong has occurred, the media outlet may agree to publish a correction or invite you to write a letter to the editor that will be published to rectify the situation. Granted, damage has been done. Hopefully, these situations are rare.

Media Consultants and Agencies

Expert counsel for dealing with the media is available and often worth the price. Depending on the in-house talent of your Communications staff, the scope of your contact with the media, and the impact that the media has on your business, it might be very worthwhile to retain a consultant or agency dedicated to media relations.

Often, consultants and agencies are retained for training executives, product launches, product line marketing, special events and crises. They should be interviewed and vetted like any other outside contractor. Selecting the right consultant or agency is competitive. Candidates are provided with the parameters and details of the requirement and invited to submit proposals or make presentations showing how they would meet your expectations. Based on what you see, hear and feel, you decide and select.

Because we live in a complicated and compartmentalized world, be aware that media consultants and agencies specialize in specific industries, such as pharmaceuticals, medical devices, defense, aviation, real estate, retail, consumer goods, food, nutrition, etc. The list goes on and even delves into segments within an industry—women's shoes, communications satellites, dog food, toys for toddlers, etc. Professional associations and your network of contacts within your industry are good places to start when shopping for a consultant or agency.

Leader's Takeaway

- The media are not the enemy. Like you, they have a job to do. When they do it well—with your help—all are well-served.
- While there always will be skepticism or tension between you and them, the media serve as the means—the intermediary—for communicating with your important external publics. Sometimes, it helps to look beyond the media to the audience they serve. That's whom you really care about.
- The more you know about the media and how they operate, the less anxiety and trouble you will have working with them.
- The more knowledgeable and skillful you are in presenting your news message, the more control you will have in shaping the news. Make sure your news releases are well-conceived and well-written, and go into interviews well-prepared and with your own agenda. Don't *just* answer the questions.
- If you have a Communications manager or department, make sure your Communications lead is media savvy and provides you with the support and coaching you should be getting.

CHAPTER 9

COMMUNITY RELATIONS

An organization has a social responsibility to make its community a better place to live and work. Your presence affects those around you. As a leader, take the initiative to be a good neighbor and have a positive impact. Think of what a great place your community would be if other organizations like yours adopted the same attitude. Be the model. It's more about taking an interest and making an effort than it is about money. If you go about it the right way, the time and effort you invest will pay dividends. Be a good citizen and reach out to your neighbors and local officials in cooperative and supportive ways.

> "Organizations have a social responsibility to be good corporate citizens beyond paying taxes and obeying laws and regulations."

Realize that many members of your organization live in nearby communities, some closer than others. You are fortunate to have them in your organization as much as they are to have you. In this respect, you enjoy a reputation as an area employer and a contributor the local economy. Imagine how the reputation of your organization would be further enhanced by being regarded as a good corporate citizen.

Who Is in Your Community?

Think broadly. Community is not determined just by proximity and town lines. It also involves common interests and serving the greater good. Consider how your activities affect people in your community and how they affect and support your operation. We're talking about:

- immediate neighbors left and right, above and below you, and down the road—physical proximity
- local police and fire departments, EMT and ambulance services—emergency services
- healthcare providers and the nearby hospital—medical services
- your mayor, town and village council, administrators, and departments
- merchants and the Chamber of Commerce
- state and federal representatives and agencies
- utility providers—electricity, gas, water
- other service providers and suppliers
- schools and colleges in your area
- civic, volunteer and charitable organizations in your area, such as the United Way, Red Cross, Salvation Army, YMCA, youth programs, food pantries, and others
- Professional associations comprised of other organizations in the same or related industries as yours

The Cost Can Be Negligible

Establishing and maintaining good community relations doesn't necessarily translate to big bucks. It's sort of like wearing a smile or saying something nice to someone. It doesn't cost anything (or much). You just have look around and think to do it. How? Volunteerism is one way.

Encourage employees to volunteer in the community. Where? At their children's schools, in youth or scouting programs, at their churches, and in civic organizations. Chances are many people in your organization already volunteer. For others, an encouraging word from the boss may be all it takes.

Recognize people who volunteer. Put their names and photos on a special bulletin board, in an e-newsletter or printed version, on your website, or even in your annual report. Provide a free lunch or gift certificate to a local restaurant to the volunteer of the month. Recognize volunteers with a kind word, a handwritten note, or a certificate suitable for framing. When it catches on that volunteering is encouraged and recognized in your organization, you'll be surprised at just how much people can do. Note that while most people like to be recognized for what they do, some prefer to remain anonymous or private about their volunteer activities. Honor it.

Appoint a Community Relations Manager or Coordinator

If you're big enough, find an outgoing and engaging person in your organization and appoint him or her as your Community Relations manager/coordinator/representative/liaison, either as a primary or secondary responsibility within Communications or Human

Resources. Have that person identify and prioritize which publics are important to your organization and establish a plan or a program to engage with each.

Share Community Relations Responsibilities

With or without a Community Relations manager to coordinate a program, involve your staff. Identify those with whom you want to engage, and assign others on your staff to liaise with an entity in your community. For example –

- Reserve connecting with the governor or mayor for yourself.
- Ask your chief counsel to connect with key legislators.
- Assign your head of security to establish a relationship with local law enforcement.
- Have your facility engineer connect with the fire department and utility company.

Get the idea? If you put word out that you are looking to employees or members of your organization to connect on your behalf with various community organizations, you might be surprised that relationships already exist. Just be careful that you select the right person and provide guidelines for what you want the relationship to be. This could be a good project for your Communications director or Community Relations manager.

Once relationships are established, invite one, two or three key community leaders or influencers in monthly for breakfast or lunch, give them an overview of your organization, walk them around, and hear what they do and what their concerns and challenges are.

Cultivate Relationships

Relationships don't happen overnight or automatically. They take someone's initiative and time to develop. A first contact is a beginning. Don't let it be the last or a one-time event. Follow up. Keep the relationship going with a note or a phone call: "Thanks for stopping by. Good meeting you. Let's do it again. How about showing me around your place?"

When you know someone and then need that person's help for something, it tends to go better than meeting for the first time. Imagine having to call the police or fire department to your facility for an incident when you or a member of your staff has an established professional relationship with the chief. You'll be in a better place to deal with each other and the situation because you have a rapport, a relationship, a respect for one another, and an appreciation for the other's position and interests.

Sponsorship

Businesses and organizations are targets for nonprofits, charities and community projects. The impression is that businesses have deep pockets and budgets for charitable giving and sponsorship. This is not always the case. But if you can, carve out a small part of your budget for community support.

Establish Guidelines for Giving

Establish parameters for giving. If there is an obvious connection, tie your support and contributions to the type of business you are or the work you do. If there is not an obvious tie, designate the type(s) of activities you will support. Parameters can include more than one category with percentages assigned. Parameters for giving might include considering requests that support:

- local education
- STEM—science, technology, engineering, math
- scouting
- youth athletics
- elderly services
- the arts, such as a local theater
- health care: a hospital, a clinic, hospice, children's health, etc.
- local humane society or animal shelter
- food kitchen or food pantry for those in need
- … and many other possibilities; your call

There are many worthy causes within our communities. No individual, business, or organization can be expected to support them all. By establishing parameters for giving, you make it known what types of activities you will support within limits, and it gives your organization guidelines or criteria for deciding to support certain causes and not others.

Some organizations establish boards or committees that involve officers and employees to review requests and decide what will be honored and for how much. If you go this route, it's a good idea to have representatives from Human Resources, Legal and Communications (your Community Relations manager) on the board, along with representatives from other departments. Also, in some organizations, leaders reserve some funds for discretionary or unplanned "must-do" community support.

Supporting Education and Schools

Education in general and schools at all levels offer numerous opportunities for reaching into the community in various ways. These can include:

- donating no-longer-needed computers, furniture, and audio-visual equipment
- scholarships, or scholarships for the children of employees
- paid and unpaid internships
- summer jobs for students *and* teachers
- providing speakers for career fairs
- encouraging employees to volunteer as tutors—even allowing tutoring for one or two hours a week on company time
- if manufacturing or fabricating, coordinating with community and technical colleges for training specific to company requirements, thus creating a potential path to employment or a pipeline for trained workers
- matching employee contributions to schools, colleges and universities

Speakers' Bureau

Depending on interest and reach, your organization might consider establishing a formal or informal speakers' bureau. This involves offering or advertising the availability of speakers from your organization to civic organizations, schools, and conferences. Your Community Relations manager would maintain a list of speakers and their topics, and coordinate details. Organizations that have more formal speakers' bureaus sometimes align with a local chapter of Toastmasters

International. More often, it is an informal arrangement in which a Community Relations manager knows who enjoys speaking and is good at it. If speakers talk about the organization, there needs to be review and approval process in place to ensure only authorized subject matter is presented. A speakers' bureau represents a nice outreach opportunity that can reflect well on an organization.

Professional Associations

Professionals belong to professional associations.[42] This goes both for the organization itself as a corporate entity and for individuals who are or aspire to be professionals in their respective fields. Advantages of membership include:

- staying abreast of trends and developments in your field
- validating you and your organization as a serious player in your industry
- offering opportunities for training, seminars and conferences
- connecting with colleagues and talent in your field
- sharing new ideas and solutions to challenges in your field

As a leader, you can further capitalize personally by:

- staying abreast of developments by reading or writing for association publications
- participating on a committee relevant to your business interests
- being an association officer for a term or two
- participating in association meetings and conferences

See chapter 5 for a partial list of professional associations related to the communications field. What professional associations exist in your field or industry that would be beneficial for you or your organization to be a member?

Community Relations offers tangible and intangible benefits. What is presented are merely suggestions to get you thinking about what's right, what's realistic, what's of interest or benefit to you and your organization, and how you could be a contributing member in your community with or without investing a lot of time and money. Granted, everyone's situation is different. It boils down to a matter of attitude. Do you think an organization has a role in its community? How much of an effort are you willing to make?

Leader's Takeaway

- Organizations have a social responsibility to be good corporate citizens beyond paying taxes and obeying laws and regulations.
- Having a Community Relations mindset and program, formal or informal, offers benefits to all parties.
- It's great if you can allocate a slice of your budget to Community Relations, but you can still have a viable program with little or no funding.

CHAPTER 10

DIGITAL AND SOCIAL MEDIA

The Internet and rise of social media have changed the game about how people get their information and interact—a statement of the obvious. But there are still lingering thoughts by a few who think surfing websites and spending time on social media platforms are a distraction, frivolous, and an abuse of company time. Especially for astute business people and well-informed citizens who know where to go and how to work with the tools that technology has given us, being "plugged in" is essential for survival. Working purposefully, the savvy person with a smartphone or laptop can cover more ground and accomplish more before 12 noon than the most experienced road warrior could in a month.

Granted, nothing beats face-to-face meetings—a handshake, a lunch together, getting a feel about someone's interest, understanding where he or she is coming from. However, time and distance limit what is possible. By harnessing the advantages that social media has enabled, relationships can be cultivated to more meaningful, deeper and more productive levels. Don't pass up opportunities to meet in person. At the same time, capitalize on the speed, reach and efficiency that social media platforms provide to stay connected whenever appropriate and not be dependent on "until we meet again" to sustain and improve a relationship with an individual or a group.

Since the advent of the Internet and social media, leaders now have more channels than ever before to send and receive—a good thing. Surely your Communications and Sales and Marketing staff are using capabilities that various social media platforms provide. As a leader, so should you. If not, get a coach—from Communications, Information Technology, or Human Resources—to show you the possibilities until you are comfortable going solo. Let's look at a few ways for you to participate if you are not already engaged.

Your Organization's Website

One no-brainer is the decision to maintain an excellent website. It is your public brochure—a look into your organization that is as fundamental as your mailing address and telephone number. Don't underestimate and take for granted its importance. While others maintain it, you as a leader have a responsibility to make sure your website is an accurate representation of your organization. Prospects will look at your website before ever deciding whether they want to speak with you or someone in your organization. When was the last time you looked at your organization's website? Take a look and ask yourself, does it say the things you want said? Does it reflect how you want your organization perceived? Does it do a good job of telling your story? Are you maximizing its full potential, or is it just out there? If you haven't reviewed it in a while, it will be an hour well spent going through your website and asking a few simple questions. Is your website …

- **Accurate?** Does it tell the story of who you are, what you do, and what you offer in terms of solutions, products and services, or is it just a dry, boring catalog of information, facts and figures?

- **User-friendly?** Pretend you are a customer or client and go look for information that you think they would be looking for. How easy or hard is it to navigate and find the information? How many clicks does it take, or how deep into the website do you have to go?

- **Content rich?** Why would people visit your website in the first place? Again, put yourself in the shoes of a visitor to your website and ask yourself whether it's informative and helpful. Is your website *content rich,* meaning, does it deliver high-quality substance—"the beef"? Is it current and updated? Granted, deciding what to include and what to hold back is a double-edge sword. Hold back too much and potential customers skip to the next website. Put too much out there, and you run the risk of giving away a competitive advantage. Tough call; opt for more rather than less.

- **Copy heavy?** Writing for websites is different from other types of writing. People don't read webpages; they glance and scan. Grey blocks of copy—series of sentences and paragraphs—are discouraging and largely go unread. Instead, viewers look for key words in headlines, subheads, bullet phrases, and images. "Hey, we're not the readers we used to be, and we're in a hurry!"

- **Visually appealing?** Pictures and words working together tell stories. Pictures include photos, charts, diagrams, illustrations and maps. Does your website effectively use visuals and words that complement one another, are attractively arranged, and tell your story?

- **Displaying keywords?** Keywords are especially important on websites. Search engines use keywords to steer viewers and potential customers to information on websites. What are the buzzwords or phrases that capture what's hot in your field or the uniqueness of your organization? Are they visible in the right places? Is a knowledgeable person in your organization periodically reviewing and updating keywords as products, services and priorities change to help search engines steer traffic to your website? Ask your staff about *search engine optimization* (SEO) to increase traffic.

- **Overloaded?** The opposite of *content rich* and related to *copy heavy.* Is your website loaded with extraneous information that doesn't contribute to a better understanding of the organization from the perspective of an outsider? Many organizations overload their websites simply because they can. Have a rationale for everything on your website. Unnecessary information gets in the way of what is relevant and important, and it discourages searchers from looking further. Analyze hits and page visits to see what people are interested in. Eliminate or reduce content that is not viewed, or make it more interesting or relevant. Have a place where a visitor can ask for what's not on your website: "I'm interested in xyz. What are your capabilities in this area?" And be sure to answer promptly.

- **Dynamic?** Frequent changes and updates keep your website fresh and interesting, and encourage repeat visits. Even though content remains king, fresh news and information, color, good photos, videos, and links to interesting and relevant sources keep people coming back. Highlight changes. When was the last time new information was posted on your website? Was it prominently featured or buried somewhere?

- **People oriented?** Does your website communicate a human dimension? Are people shown performing and making contributions? Beyond leaders, do you feature individuals in short vignettes for their special talents? Does your website tell any stories about customers and how they use your products and services? People are what make organizations successful and give them personality. Does your website show signs of life?

- **A one-way proposition?** Too many websites are. Make sure your website has feedback mechanisms that are in the right places, easy to use, monitored daily, and answered promptly. Being responsive is an indication of your organization's true concern for its customers and the service they can expect. If digital and social media, websites included, are anything, they are about connecting, dialoguing, cultivating relationships, and responding to wishes and wants. Ask for a report of website traffic and inquiries, responses provided, and the dates and times of each. If you are getting little traffic or there is lag time between requests and responses, your website is not doing the job.

- **Competitive?** How does your website compare to those of your competitors or other organizations similar to yours? Which is a better experience? In addition to the intelligence you can glean from other websites, what can you borrow or imitate from them that would make your website more interesting and effective?

These and more are questions you can ask yourself and those responsible for maintaining your organization's website. Of course, consultants and agencies abound that will evaluate your website and make recommendations to improve it, or do it all for you—but first, give it a going-over yourself. You'll find it to be a revealing and useful exercise.

Other Uses

While your website is your flagship digital presence and identity, there are other ways you can communicate on the Internet as part or independent of your website. They include:

- Blog: A blog is like a column published in a newspaper or magazine, except that it is digital and appears on the Internet. It can be part of or linked to a website, confined to an organization's intranet for its employees only, or available on the Internet as an independent mini-website. Just as a column appears at regular intervals, say weekly, a blog is similarly posted as a series. Postings are filed in reverse chronological order, are indexed, and can be researched. A blog is a terrific way for a leader to communicate with his or her organization on a regular basis on one or several topics, upcoming challenges, issues, priorities—you decide. If you are too busy to write on a topic yourself, use a ghostwriter to draft it and then edit the piece to give it your personal touch, style or emphasis.
- Podcast: A podcast is a digital media file that can be downloaded, stored and viewed on a computer, tablet or smartphone. It can be text, audio or video, and it usually addresses one subject. As leader, you could use it to welcome new employees (which you should do in person unless you are very large or widely distributed); introduce or emphasize a policy, such as mutual respect, safety, or compliance; or address a

workplace problem, such as breakdowns or quality issues. It's a mini-program that can be viewed as needed and at a time convenient for the viewer.

- Webcast: A webcast is a live broadcast—video and sound—of an event transmitted over the Internet. Like a live television program broadcasted over the airwaves, cable or satellite, it is a one-way proposition. Publicly traded companies use webcasts for quarterly reports to investors and use an open phone line or another work-around for questions and discussion. For a leader with a dispersed workforce, a webcast is a good vehicle for quarterly or semi-annual updates, introduction of a new product or service, and announcing significant changes in policy and procedures.

- Webinar: A webinar, also referred to as web conferencing, can be a meeting, seminar or conference conducted over the Internet. It's live and interactive, and it can accommodate text, slides, voice and video. Companies with distant locations or employees working remotely have been web conferencing for years. Vendors, such as your telephone, cable and Internet providers, offer web conferencing services for smaller outfits who don't have in-house capabilities. Topics appropriate for webinars or web conferencing are unlimited: connecting sales representatives in widely separated territories or Human Resources representatives at different facilities, planning trade show strategy, bringing Sales and Marketing together for the rollout of a new product or service, changing or implementing a new process, procedure or policy, implementing a new law or regulation, bringing a new team on-board ... the possibilities are endless.

Your Information Technology and Communications departments have the know-how to implement these channels and more. It's routine business for them. Equipment and software are mature. If you don't already know, find out or ask for a briefing on how your organization is using ways to connect over the web and whether the capabilities are being maximized.

Social Media: May the Force Be with You

Social media is a collective term for communications platforms in which participants provide the content and interact with single individuals, friends, groups with common interests in defined areas, or a large public sphere. Advances in the technology combined with relatively low costs have enabled this sociological phenomenon we call social media to connect individuals and give them voice for everything from idle banter to matters of importance. Think of social media as a conversation taking place among friends and family, as well as at school and work, or among people with common interests about work, social issues, politics, hobbies, sports, science, and local, national and world events. You name it—there is an ongoing conversation. Mobile devices in our hands, pockets and pocketbooks—always within reach—with capabilities for voice, text, photography and video provide instant connectivity and make each of us a potential news source and broadcaster of whatever is happening around us. It's proving to be both a blessing and a curse for its capabilities. One thing is for sure: it's here, and it's not going away.

From a leader's perspective, recognize that social media is a powerful force. It provides leaders with the tools to directly connect with virtually every person and public in the leader's universe. It also represents an opportunity to learn what is on people's minds and what they think of you and your organization. Social media is a means to exercise leadership provided the leader sees its potential, develops a strategy, and has the desire to make it work. Don't be a leader with your head in the sand. Be a player, and with staff support, use social media to connect, establish relationships, converse, listen, and respond appropriately.

SOCIAL MEDIA PLATFORMS[43]

TYPE	EXAMPLES, DESCRIPTION
Social Networking	Facebook, Twitter, LinkedIn
Blogs	Personal websites – regular postings on a topic, field or interest…like a column in a publication
Video and image sharing	YouTube, SlideShare, Instagram, Flickr
Chat rooms, message boards	Places where people meet online and discuss topics of interest, anyone can start one
Review sites	Yelp, TripAdvisor, Angie's list, Amazon, Rotten Tomatoes
Listservs	Email messages sent to members who have signed up for a common interest or subject
Wikis	Websites where anyone can edit, add, update
Social bookmarking	Users suggest interesting content to others–StumbleUpon, Digg
Mobile applications	GPS – generated located services – routing, directions, where to find places like gas stations, restaurants…you name it

David Meerman Scott, *The New Rules of Marketing & PR, John Wiley & Sons, Inc.*, Hoboken, New Jersey, 2015 pp. 55-56

Why Social Media?

If you have doubts about why participating on social media platforms is worth the time and effort of a leader, consider the capabilities it provides.

- **Cultivating relationships:** Social media provides a means for establishing and deepening a leader's relationship with customers, prospects, employees, and others. It takes a leader beyond the cold business of seller-buyer and boss-subordinate. Embedded in a relationship are attributes of trust and respect that are earned over time. Social media present a leader and his or her organization with countless opportunities to cultivate these attributes, whether it is suggesting a solution, sharing information, saying congratulations, offering help, or just showing interest.

- **Instantly targeting and reaching prospects, customers, subordinates and other important publics:** With nearly everyone in possession of a smartphone or close to a laptop, virtually everyone with whom a leader wishes or needs to be in contact is just a few clicks away. Social media offers instant connectivity. A leader no longer must wait for the next opportunity to communicate—for the next news release, the next issue, the next meeting, or the next time he or she sees someone. And the message arrives quickly, unfiltered by editors, intermediaries and gatekeepers. Whether it is one person or a specific group, or whether the receiver is in his or her office, traveling, or in the field, connecting is easier than it's ever been—a good thing!

- **Participating in the conversation:** A continuous conversation is taking place on social media.[44] The challenge for the leader is to find where relevant and important discussions are taking place and join the conversation. If you perceive yourself or your organization to be, or desire to be, an important player in a given field, then you don't want to be left out of the conversation. Your staff should be monitoring various social media platforms, searching for relevant conversations on websites, blogs and chatrooms, and making recommendations as to where and how to engage. If you or your organization were ever the subject of discussion for good or bad reasons, it would be unfortunate if someone from your organization didn't jump in with a comment or perspective. When you do engage, make sure you are contributing substance and not just more noise.

- **Shaping the conversation:** Beyond participating in the conversation, social media offers the opportunity to *shape* the conversation by introducing topics, challenges and issues and offering ideas, thoughts and solutions. Social media provides an opportunity to demonstrate *thought leadership* in your field. People, organizations and potential customers are attracted to others whom they perceive to be engaged, dynamic, forward-thinking and solutions oriented.

- **Listening to what is being said:** Social media also provides honest, unfiltered ways for you to hear or see what your customers are saying about you as a leader, your organization, and your products and services. This can be humbling and frustrating at times. It is also essential that deficiencies be identified, evaluated, and improved or fixed. Your reputation and success depend on it. If there are pockets of discrimination, fraud, waste, sexual harassment, safety infractions, noncompliance, cutting corners and other abuses within your organization, you stand a good chance of finding out about them on social media. Monitoring what people are saying also provides an opportunity to engage with people important to your organization, clarify misconceptions, identify holes in your marketing, and learn about interests in new issues or technology, or what a competitor is doing. In other words, hearing the chatter on social media can be a tremendous source of intelligence.

Make Social Media Work for You

Use social media with purpose. When you know its capabilities, devise a social media strategy with objectives—the *what* part—and a tactical plan to achieve them—the *how* part. Here are three suggestions:

- Create a position for a Digital and Social Media manager within your Communications department if your organization can support it. If not, make it a duty of the person performing the Communications function with the following responsibilities:
    o Develop, monitor and update a social media strategy, plan and policy for your organization.
    o Develop and update a dynamic and content-rich website.
    o Make a recommendation for which social media platforms the organization should participate in, and develop a presence for each.
    o Monitor and report what conversations are taking place about the organization, its people, and its products and services.
    o Identify industry opportunities and trends found online and in social media.
    o Visit competitor, supplier and other relevant websites for news, trends, and new products and services.
    o Identify, encourage and assist leaders' participation on blogs, podcasts, webinars and other appropriate places.
    o Ensure feedback and two-way mechanisms are in place and functioning.

- o Share, collaborate in and support social media activity with Sales and Marketing, Human Resources and other departments.
- Develop news and content adaptable for your website and different social media platforms. One size does not fit all. For example, when issuing a news release about a new product or service, rewrite or repackage the news, making it appropriate for other uses to achieve maximum impact.
  - o Typically, a news release is posted on the news tab or page of your website.
  - o Put a teaser on your website's home page that a new release has just been posted.
  - o Post the news release on the organization's intranet, ensuring that employees see it, are informed, and can retransmit and talk about it with their contacts.
  - o On Twitter, send out a tweet with a link to your organization's news page.
  - o Just as you would do for reporters and editors at traditional media outlets, email or send a link of the news release to bloggers who are interested in what you do.
  - o Repackage the news release with a photo and caption or video for posting Facebook, Instagram, YouTube and other platforms.
  - o Create talking points about the new news for leaders and others to use and incorporate in their remarks as opportunities arise.
- Cultivate a relationship with bloggers. Understand that some bloggers enjoy rock-star status for their influence in certain fields. They are respected for their knowledge and independence. It's similar to the difference between editorial content

and advertising. One carries the implication of objectivity, the other subjectivity. Find out who the influential bloggers are in your field. Once they are identified by you or your staff, stay close to them without pandering.

- o If bloggers have an interest in your organization, make sure they are on your media contact list.
- o Dialogue with bloggers, letting them know who you are and where your interests lie.
- o Above all, bloggers appreciate substantive new information. In addition to news releases, feed them anything you have, come across, and can share that is relevant to your mutual interests, i.e., research, white papers, articles, links. The more good information you provide, the more they will pay attention to you. Conversely, understand that weak and self-promoting information will undermine your credibility and influence.

Leader's Takeaway

- Take an hour to review your organization's website. Make sure it is content-rich, properly represents your organization, and answers the mail from the perspective of a visitor.
- Don't underestimate the power and potential of social media. Participate with purpose. Harness its reach, speed and ability to deliver your message and cultivate deeper relationships.

CHAPTER 11

BRANDING AND ADVERTISING

Books are written on branding. Here it is in a nutshell. Branding is managing your organization's reputation in the broadest sense. It is multifaceted and manifested in physical and psychological ways. The objectives of branding are to be regarded as the *recognized leader* and *preferred solution* for whatever you do, to build a *relationship* that runs deeper than any one product, and to build a long-term loyalty. Think broadly across all aspects of your business or organization when you think about maintaining your brand. It involves everything from your name and logo to dependability and customer service.[45]

> "Branding involves everything from your name and logo to dependability and customer service."

Good branding depends on effective communications. Just as with other reasons for communicating, a lot depends on how your message is received and reinforced over time. This requires listening to customer concerns and wishes, fixing problems, reacting quickly, maintaining good working relationships, and predicting future needs. If you are thinking one thing and your customer is thinking something else, or if you have a better opinion of yourself than others do, then you are missing the mark.

To better understand what branding is, think of the *feeling* you get when you see or hear the names Coca-Cola, Apple, IBM, Toyota, YMCA, Mercedes-Benz, John Deere, Habitat for Humanity, and United States Marine Corps—all examples of strong brands. It's recognition and acknowledgement of the brand in its respective market that goes beyond a product or characteristic. Branding includes:

- **Recognition:** a look and feel that stand out and are unmistakable. It starts with your logo and extends to design, style, colors, signage, motifs and every visible representation. Strong brands have style guides that govern details, such as business cards, type style, fonts, color palettes, stationery, logo size and placement for every conceivable situation, inside and outside signage, and sometimes even furniture and carpet. You name it—there is a brand standard.

- **Leadership:** the perception that your company or organization is the leader in its field. If not the leader, then the up-and-comer, or the spoiler, or the problem-solver, or the most reliable, or the oldest and most experienced, or the visionary—whatever unique space you wish to claim and the market buys into.

- **Reliability:** the confidence that when you engage, sign on, or buy this brand, you have the peace of mind that you know what you're getting, that it is the best value for the price, and that it is tried and true.

- **Consistency:** the knowledge that every product and service meets the same high standard, is as good as the one before and the one after, for every customer, and that it will perform as promised.

Another aspect of building a strong brand within your market or industry is the goal of establishing a trusted relationship with your customer or client. "Why would I change? They're the best. They've taken care of me in the past, and they'll take care of me in the future." This sounds like how my father felt about Ford in the 1950s. This kind of brand loyalty requires that everyone in the organization understand his or her role to maintain and uphold the brand. When you meet with your staff and employees, talk about brand building and maintenance—how important it is for your position in the marketplace and your ultimate success. Also talk about how it can be undermined or damaged.

One caution: In building your brand, looking inward, don't forget about the customer, looking outward. Don't be so focused on brand maintenance that you compromise or sacrifice customer service. The brand is not the end in itself. It is the formula to long-term and continued success in the marketplace. If your branding is strong and well-managed, this conflict will not occur because a satisfied customer is your goal.[46]

Advertising

Word of mouth—a strong recommendation from a trusted friend or respected colleague—is the best form of advertising. This form of advertising cannot be bought. If you learn that you made a sale or earned some new business resulting from a kind word from a satisfied customer, it certainly would be worth a *thank you* to that person and maybe even a discount on a future transaction. But, understanding that you must work for every cent and grow, advertising is a necessary marketing vehicle to make sales and attract new business.

"Word of mouth is the best form of advertising, and it cannot be bought."

The primary purpose of advertising is *to sell* your product or service. It is an important element in the branding equation, along with making quality products and providing excellent customer service. Advertising works best when it is targeted to an audience, public, readership, and viewer who by demographics, profession, field, position or interest are likely prospects to purchase the product or service. The more precisely you can pinpoint who prospective customers are and provide a solution or fill a want, the more effective your advertising will be, wherever it's placed—be it in publications (newspapers and magazines), on websites and social media platforms, on television and radio, and in places where your prospect goes, such as public transportation centers, busy thoroughfares, theaters, concerts, and sporting and civic events.

Other terms used to describe targeted advertising include *direct, precision* and *database* advertising. The more you know about your prospects, the better able you are to tailor your selling message and place your ad. In this respect, the demographic information gleaned from profiles as individuals establish social media accounts, make purchases, and click on selected websites is very useful for targeting groups with similar interests.

Where to Advertise

Perhaps the biggest and most difficult question to answer is *where to advertise*. Advertising is expensive, and budgets are never enough to cover everywhere your ads could or should be. The more you know about your target audience and the places where you can advertise, the better decisions you and your staff can make about where to spend your never-enough advertising dollars for maximum impact. Considerations for developing an advertising plan include:

- **Know who your target audience is.** Whether it is consumer or business-to-business advertising, the principle is the same: The more you know about your prospective customer, the more effective your advertising will be. Take your advertising to where they congregate.

- **Go direct.** Go directly to your prospective customer if you have good contact information. Advertising on social media has the capability and sophistication to send ads directly to individuals based on their profile information, purchasing patterns, demonstrated interests, and any criteria you specify. Even direct mail (snail mail) is more effective and personal than indirect advertising serving broad audiences, such as newspapers and billboards.

- **Diversify.** Advertise in different media. Mix it up by allocating resources to traditional, online and social media. This is not a contradiction to *go direct*. For the same reason that preferences and habits govern where individuals go for news, the same principle applies to their exposure to advertising. Although the trend for getting news and information is shifting more and more to online and social media, people are still reading newspapers and magazines and getting their news from television and radio. Don't count them out. And most traditional media outlets—i.e., print and broadcast—now have online editions and may offer discounts and packages for advertising in both print and online editions.

- **Study media kits.** A standard tool for selling advertising is the advertiser's media kit, delivered in a nice folder with tabbed inserts and online often as a PDF file. The media kit contains valuable information about the advertiser's editorial focus, departments, editorial calendar, circulation, and reader or viewer profiles. It also contains information about technical specifications and costs for one-off and multiple ad buys. The circulation and profile information provided are audited, attempting to validate its worthiness as the preferred place to advertise. Media kits provide a wealth of information that the diligent media planner uses to create spreadsheets to compare data and make recommendations about where to advertise and how much to invest.

- **Consult media outlet representatives.** Every media kit is delivered by a sales representative from the media outlet. Make no mistake—their job is to sell ads. Even so, they are valuable sources of information about your market. They pay attention to what is happening in your industry, and they meet with your counterparts in other companies. If a good match, they can make suggestions and offer packages to help you get the most from your investment. Most media outlet sales representatives are well-connected and knowledgeable. It's a good idea to include them in your network of professional contacts and meet with them whenever you can—something a good media manager does routinely.

- **Measure results and experiment.** Once advertising has been placed, track the number of inquiries and leads an ad generates and see if they convert to actual sales. Understand that no one ad is going to close a sale, but it is part of the sales equation. Still, an ad may be enough to pique interest and start the ball rolling. If measured results are inconclusive or disappointing, move your advertising to other places.

- **Talk with customers.** A great deal of information can be gained by purposeful listening. As you and your sales representatives travel about and meet with prospects and existing customers, listen or gently probe for information on how or where they heard about you, your organization, or your product. Was it an ad, an article, someone's recommendation, or another source? Take note of what publications are on your customer's desk or the table in the outer office or lobby. Meet with customers at trade shows and observe how they engage with you and others. In other words, always be listening and watching. Little bits of information here and there can paint a picture that can tell you a lot.

- **Track competitors' advertising.** Pay attention to where your competitors are advertising. Assuming they are also diligent in their research and careful with their spending, the placement of their ads may be a tip-off to a market opportunity that you and your planners overlooked.

Creating the Ad

Leave creating the ad to the pros—either the in-house graphics department or outside agencies. Provide detailed guidance; then back off and let them do their job. Agencies specialize, know what sells and where, and are experts in design. This doesn't mean you shouldn't be involved, but give them license to be creative without micromanaging or breathing down their necks. Working with good designers and copywriters, you won't be disappointed.

Once you've done your part, your ad developers should come back to you with a few different concept proposals—*comps* in agency speak—for your consideration, reaction and further guidance for the next round. The number of comps and rounds of comps should be specified in the request for proposal or purchase order.

Copy Development: Pitch Benefits, Not Features

When determining what an ad should say, take the perspective of the buyer or the customer. As objectively as you can, ask yourself how the buyer will benefit from purchasing your product or service. The tendency of sellers is to want to brag about and sell nifty new features that may distinguish or differentiate the product or service from the competition. Pointing out what is different from the other guy's is important, but do it in terms that benefit the customer. You are talking about the same things, but the perspective is different. A good copy-writer knows the difference. Perspective is more than semantics. As an example of selling benefits, think of a selling a car's navigation system.

- If you were selling *features,* you would emphasize the newer high-fidelity, two- or three-dimensional display in your choice of colors, showing alternate routes—most direct, fastest, other ways to get there, and the time it takes for each.
- If you are selling *benefits,* you would emphasize that the system can be configured to how you prefer to see your route displayed and what's easiest for you to see, understand and follow—two or three dimensional—and your route choice

depending on your situation today: are you in a hurry to get there, or do you want to go another way for a change?

Related to selling benefits, not features, don't overwhelm an ad with too much information. Sometimes ad copy is overloaded with too many details. Make a good case for one, two, or not more than three of your most compelling selling points couched as benefits, and resist burying the viewer in every detail. Trust that the design of visuals (photos or art) working with your carefully chosen words will be compelling enough without saying everything that could be said. Include a website address that contains everything else. The serious prospect will either see the possibilities or seek them out.

Call to Action

A well-designed ad concludes with a strong *call to action*—the next step. After the ad copy has made its pitch, it needs to convert the customer's heightened interest to action. Including a link to a website for more information encourages a customer to safely investigate further without being bothered by a pesky or pushy sales rep. Make sure the website picks up where the ad ends and delivers more details, such as technical information or potential applications for the product or service. Don't leave a customer hanging—"Looks interesting, so now what?" End with a strong *call to action*.

In addition to including a website, encourage follow-up action with:

- an 800 number—but make sure the person who answers is primed and ready

- the name of a real person, telephone number and email address—again, a knowledgeable person
- an invitation to visit you at an upcoming trade show, booth #123, or hospitality suite
- "Come by for the demonstration" (or test drive)
- promise of a white paper, copy of interesting article, or relevant research
- offer of modest gift—an umbrella, a windbreaker—or a chance in a raffle for a more substantial gift—round-trip airplane tickets for two anywhere in the continental US

Image Advertising

Although advertising is primarily a selling mechanism, occasionally an organization will place an ad to enhance its image, espouse a position, defend an action, or endorse a candidate. In image advertising, you are selling yourself and paying for position to ensure being seen. It is an attempt to make a powerful statement. It also recognizes that the organization's message might not pass editorial scrutiny, be buried deep within, or be edited to its bare bones, and therefore, not give the organization the opportunity to say what it wants to say and in the manner it wants it said. Buying a page for a premium position is an expensive way to make a point. Alternatives include submitting a well-crafted letter to the editor or an opinion piece, understanding that these are subject to acceptance and editing.

Budgeting and the Cost of Advertising

Advertising is expensive. Therefore, targeting is so important. The better you target, the greater the return on investment. Various models exist for determining what an advertising budget should be, but all are *guesstimates* unless you have historical data to support how much advertising generates X amount of sales. Suffice to say, advertise as much as you can afford, but do it smartly.

Methods for determining what your advertising budget should be include:

- percentage of sales
- unit of sales
- objective and task
- historical
- match the competition
- all you can afford
- seat of the pants
- combinations of the above[47]

A study by the Strategic Planning Institute (SPI) of Cambridge, Massachusetts, suggests other guidelines to help determine advertising budget.[48] They include:

- The higher your company's market share, the more you should spend on advertising.
- Companies launching new products should spend more on advertising than companies with mature or old products.
- Fast-growing markets typically require higher ad expenditures.

- Advertising expenditures need to be higher when a large amount of your plant's production capacity is underused.
- High levels of advertising and promotion are required for "low-ticket" items.
- The less your product represents as a percentage of the customer's total purchases, the greater the advertising and sales promotion expenditures.
- Products at both the low and high ends of the price range (discount and premium products) require higher ad expenditures.
- High quality products typically require higher advertising expenditures.
- Broad product lines typically require higher advertising expenditures.
- Standard "off-the-shelf" products require higher levels of advertising expenditures than custom products.

Obstacles in Budgeting

Those charged with executing advertising face two formidable obstacles. The first is that the person with the authority to approve the advertising budget (Is that you?) lacks an appreciation of its value. He or she views advertising as an expense, even a luxury, not an investment and a necessary cost of doing business.

Second, when business conditions take a downturn, marketing and advertising budgets are among the first items cut—again, not necessary, expendable—when quite the opposite is true. This is a time when advertising needs to be protected or even increased. If anything, scrutinize your advertising—are your ads effective and in the right places? Granted, these are hard decisions and a tough sell to executives who don't understand that sales activities, advertising among them, need to be ramped up, not reduced.

Don't Forget the Cost of Ad Development

Advertising has two cost elements: the space or time you are reserving and production of the ad itself. The second element is often forgotten or underestimated in budgeting. If you outsource ad production, plan carefully to get the most out of production costs. Consider the following options:

- inviting agencies to compete and bid on ad development to get the best value and creativity
- getting an estimate for a specified number of conceptual designs (comps)
- specifying a schedule for delivery of comps and the final ad
- complying with branding standards
- designing the same ad for different sizes and formats
- ordering film to ensure high-fidelity reproduction
- anticipating copy and graphic changes
- transitioning to the next ad

Quantity Buys Stretch Budgets

Like buying almost anything, buying ad space or time *in quantity*— for multiple placements—is less expensive than buying ads *individually*. Signing up to advertise on a regular schedule over the course of year will result in substantial savings compared to buying ads one at a time or month-to-month. Not only is it less expensive, but you also get better positioning.

Price Is Based on Size and Position

The price of an ad is based on the size of the ad (in print, full page or fractional page—half, quarter, etc.) and where the ad appears. In print publications, a half-page ad is not half the price of a full-page ad; it is more like two-thirds the price. In the electronic environment, price is determined by where the ad is placed (on the home page or deeper on the website) or when it pops up.

Choice or premium positioning costs more. Placing an ad on the inside of the front cover of a print publication *(cover 2,* in trade talk) is more expensive than on interior pages. Same for the inside back cover *(cover 3)* and the back cover *(cover 4).* If your ad appears on the interior page of a print publication or website, negotiate to have it placed on the same page as or on a facing page to one that contains an article relevant to your business. Ad space on website home pages is more expensive than follow-on pages a click or two away. If there is a department in a publication or tab on the website, such as *new products,* and your ad is introducing a new product, that section would be a logical place for an ad to appear, underscoring the importance of familiarity with the publication or website.

A final point on placement: while it should never happen, make sure your ad does not appear opposite, next to or near a direct competitor's ad. Ad sales reps know this; so do your advertising managers, but it bears mentioning.

Look for Value-Added Opportunities

By signing up for a series of ads, you may get a free ad (buy six and the seventh is free), or you may get a free ad in a special issue, a trade show edition, or a supplement. Buying ads in quantity gives your buyer leverage to negotiate. Advertising sales reps take care of their best customers—that should be you!

Advertise Consistently and Regularly

There are many more advertising opportunities than there are available advertising dollars. Your advertising manager needs to do his or her homework deciding which media to target (print—professional, trade, public; digital—Internet, websites, social media platforms; radio—local, regional, national; television—broadcast, cable, local, regional, national; outdoor billboards, etc.) or any combination that best serves the organization's marketing interests with the available budget. To the extent that you can, try to be in the same publications or media on a regular basis rather than scatter ads in different media outlets on an irregular basis. Advertising consistently and regularly in leading media outlets for your industry makes it easier for your customers to find you. They may not need you this month, but they may next month, and, ideally, they remember seeing your ad in xyz, so they know where to look now that they need you.

In addition to your selling message, consistent and regular advertising makes a statement that your organization is a serious player in its field. Ads appearing in multiple issues and places say you are committed for the long haul—an important element of your branding strategy.

Leader's Takeaway

- Branding is building and maintaining your organization's reputation with the intention of achieving long-term benefits. It's earned recognition that goes beyond any one product. It is manifested in how the organization presents itself, serves its customers, and is perceived in its market or field.

- Advertising, an element of branding, is a selling tool. It is a marketing investment—part of the cost of doing business— and should not be regarded as a luxury to be cut or reduced during downturns. To achieve maximum effectiveness, ads need to be highly targeted, and well-conceived, produced and placed.

CHAPTER 12

TRADE SHOWS

The beauty of a trade show is that you stand a good chance of connecting with many current customers and prospects in a few days that might otherwise take three to six months to see. While attending trade shows can be exciting and full of opportunities, they are also very expensive propositions. The question is, are you and members of your organization squeezing all you can from these expensive marketing three-ring circuses? Since you've made the decision to attend, your organization needs a good plan to get the biggest bang for its buck—because big

> "While exciting and full of opportunities, trade shows are expensive and can be exhausting."

bucks are what trade shows cost. Your trade show manager knows this, but he or she often gets buried in the details and doesn't have the horsepower to direct *best practices* from others in your organization who are attending. You do. Let's look at what attending trade shows entails and talk about ways to get the most out of them.

Typically, trade show expenses include:

- reserving floor space—often done a year prior
- having a custom booth constructed, maintained, stored, and refurbished, or renting one
- shipping the booth to and from the show, then on-site assembly and disassembly
- dressing the booth—graphics, media, demos, models
- utility hookups: electricity, Internet, telephones
- developing, ordering, and shipping literature and giveaways
- advertising and article placements in tradeshow programs and dailies—weeks in advance
- renting whatever you don't ship: carpet, tables, chairs, coffeepots, tape, wire, tools, extension cords, etc.
- staffing—travel, hotels, meals, participation fees
- special events and/or a hospitality suite—planning, attending, sponsoring, hosting

You can see how quickly trade show expenses add up. Large corporations have departments that manage logistics full-time. Now you're talking salaries. Medium-size outfits may or may not have a dedicated trade show manager, and for small businesses, managing trade shows is an additional duty for a marketing, sales or public relations person. Regardless of your size, know that, in addition to the costs, planning and participating take a lot of time.

To Go or Not

Trade show management starts with deciding whether to go or not. This decision should be part of the business and budget planning a year or two in advance, whatever your planning cycle is. One reason why planning can be difficult is that some industries have many trade shows—international, national, regional, seasonal, specialty, newcomers, adjacent markets—each one claiming, "You have to be there, or you'll miss an opportunity." It's a challenge deciding which ones you really should attend.

Good reasons to attend a trade show include:

- showcase your goods and services
- launch a new product or service
- reconfirm that you are a significant market player
- cultivate current customers
- build new relationships
- see what your competitors are doing
- learn more about market developments
- access your trade press
- identify merger and acquisition opportunities
- shop for talented people

Reasons not to attend could be:

- not a good fit, not your core business or target market
- save money
- conserve resources—perhaps for a different trade show
- concentrate on other priorities
- better utilization of Sales and Marketing staff

If a decision is made *not* to exhibit at a particular trade show, be aware that it could jeopardize your organization's position in its marketplace or be read as a strategic shift in emphasis. As a minimum, it might be a good idea to have a company representative attend to have a set of eyes and ears present. This person could be a regional sales representative close to the trade show venue to minimize expenses and time away from primary duties.

Also, understand that many trade shows that convene annually assign points to companies that attend year after year. These points give repeating companies priority to select choice locations on the trade show floor. Where space and placement are important, newcomers find themselves on the fringes, under balconies, behind pillars, and sometimes in annexes where traffic is lighter.

Maximize Participation

Consider using a *before*, *during* and *after* checklist approach for planning and attending trade shows to ensure all important details are addressed and maximize your presence. After attending, refine the checklists, making them better for the next time around.

Before

- Determine specific objectives for the show—what you intend to accomplish by attending this show.
- Register as early as possible to get a good location in the exhibition hall.
- Pay attention to what comes with your registration—number of exhibitor badges, ad space, etc.
- Reserve a block of hotel rooms to get the show rate at nearby locations.
- Note deadlines for ads and article placements in the show program and dailies.

- Make appointments with trade media reporters to interview key leaders, especially if you are introducing a new product or service or have something newsworthy to announce.
- Have your advertising and articles approved and ready to go to meet deadlines.
- Review the program in advance and identify lectures and meetings you or a representative should attend that will make your smarter and keep you better informed about industry trends and developments.
- Identify your person in charge (trade show captain) and determine appropriate staffing.
- Initiate appropriate contracts and reservations if you plan to have a hospitality suite or host or sponsor a reception or dinner party.
- Send letters and emails to customers and prospects advising them of your attendance and location, telling what you will be featuring, and inviting them to visit your booth or special event.
- Make appointments with key customers and prospects for meetings, meals, or entertainment. (Time at trade shows is limited. Don't let competitors fill their limited time available, leaving you out.)
- Follow up with key people you want to see. Be persistent.
- Devise a good system for capturing contact information of visitors to your booth.
- Designate a single company spokesperson for all media contact and make this person known to all participants attending from your organization.
- Prior to show time (the night before or the morning of), hold of meeting of attendees from your organization, laying out

objectives, duties, scheduling, dress, behavior, and procedures for handling VIPs, customers, and business leads. More on this below. Also, the staff needs to know who each other are and each person's area of expertise—who is there to represent what product, project or service.

During

- Plan your time—to be at the booth for meeting and greeting, attending meetings and presentations, and cruising the exhibition hall.
- Dedicate some time to scoping out the competition—visit their booths and collect their literature.
- Attend meetings and presentations that will increase your knowledge and keep you attuned to industry trends and developments.
- Visit suppliers and subcontractors—often neglected.
- Utilize breakfasts, lunches and dinners for meeting opportunities with customers, prospects and others (arrange in advance of the trade show).
- Be diligent about capturing contact information of visitors and review daily for immediate follow-up.

After

- Hold a critique or hot wash immediately after the show closes, while observations are still fresh in your mind and before you mentally check out and move on to your next challenge. Be honest in answering: What went well? What didn't? How do you make the next trade show better? Is this a show you should attend next time around?

- Follow up on customer requests, leads and information owed promptly.
- Send thank you notes or emails to visitors to your booth ("Thanks stopping by; hope we satisfied your interest"), and don't forget to thank your staff ("Good job; appreciate your hard work and being away from home").

Trade Show Staffing

As a leader, you should know who is going to a trade show to represent your organization and why. Trade shows are hard work. They often require being on your feet for long periods. For adequate staffing, consider:

- If you expect the person who is staffing your booth to be at his or her best, that person needs relief. For a ten-foot booth, consider sending three people, enabling them to rotate every two to four hours: one working the booth; another at the booth or close by for visitor surges, restocking, in the exhibition hall making contacts, scoping competitors, or attending sessions; the third person resting or working remotely from his or her hotel room.
- If you have a larger presence, two shifts are recommended.
- If you have a large show presence, appoint an on-site person in charge (booth captain); the vice president of Sales and Marketing is a good candidate. If not a VP, it should be a

senior person who knows the company well and has authority to make decisions.

- Again, for larger outfits, a logistics person is needed to coordinate shipping to and from the show, setup, opening, closing, and securing the booth each day, fixing things, replenishing literature and giveaways, and coordinating with the exhibition hall and trade show management. Typically, this is your trade show manager.

- In addition to sales representatives working the show, it's good to have technical representation from the company. Salespeople know the market and how your product or service is a good fit for potential customers, have a relationship, and can craft or close the deal. However, technical and engineering (or product, research, project or service) staff from your organization can answer the hard questions about inner workings. Also, the opportunity for a technical person to attend a trade show allows him or her to see the market under one roof, appreciate how competitive it is, and hear what's important to customers—a chance technical employees don't normally get. Such an experience can make this person a more effective employee back at the home office, plant, shop or lab.

- Working the booth is an art. The attention of whoever is on duty should be focused outward on passerby traffic, not inward. Assign individuals who have good social skills and can start and carry on a conversation. Visitors are reluctant to interrupt booth staff who don't make eye contact or seem to be busy.

  o Encourage staff to stand on the edges of booth the with their attention outward on passerby traffic, looking for glimmers of interest—it takes a split second to detect genuine interest.

o Do not allow cell phone use or eating at the booth.

o Do not allow booth staff to perform administrative tasks, such as working on laptops, at the booth, except for restocking literature or giveaways or doing a presentation or demo for a visitor.

o Discourage conversations or clustering among booth staff members.

o Encourage standing; discourage sitting.

o For visitors who show interest, ask for a business card or collect contact information and make notes about what was talked about.

o Giveaway grabbers: Some people are just interested in collecting giveaways—trade show loot. Give them whatever you can and send them on their way.

Thought Leadership

Trade shows are also opportunities to demonstrate *thought leadership* and expertise. Sign up one of your experts or leaders to present a talk or demonstration at one of the sessions that make up the other half of a trade show, convention or annual meeting. By giving a presentation, you are establishing that person and, by association, your organization as an expert, authority, thought leader, innovator, or visionary on an aspect of your business. Offering a speaker requires:

• Far-in-advance planning—programs are put together six to twelve months in advance and require vetting.

- Having a subject or topic that is timely, significant and interesting, and that will attract an audience—something new and innovative or a new solution to an old problem.
- Having a good presenter—a recognized expert and good speaker. Provide this person with the time and support to put together a first-rate presentation and review it.

Trade Shows Are Party Time—Not If Worked Right

A misconception exists that trade shows are party time—paid vacations. Any trade show warrior will tell you working a trade show can be exhausting, even if you're not involved in setting up, breaking down, and shipping your booth. Most exhibition halls have cement floors. Standing all day, smiling, and being at your best for every visitor, even if the booth is carpeted, often leaves your legs and lower back screaming. Days are long and don't end when exhibition hours end. Typically, you head back to your hotel room, freshen up, take a hot shower or bath if you're lucky, and head out again for a round of receptions, drop-ins at a hospitality suite or two, and dinner with an old customer or new prospect. That may or may not be the end of your day, depending on what else you must do. Sounds like fun, and it can be. But two or three days of working a trade show can also wear you down.

Leader's Takeaway

- Trade shows are opportunities to connect with customers, prospects and others in your industry and to see what the rest of the industry is doing.
- For the time, resources and costs that organizations invest in trade shows, it is worth a leader's time to stay informed and participate in preparatory decisions to maximize the benefits of attending. "Tell me what we're doing at the show next week" is too little, too late.
- In preparing to attend a trade show, using the *before, during* and *after* checklist approach to make sure important details are covered and opportunities are maximized.
- If it is well planned and executed, working a trade show requires long, tiring days for those representing your organization. They may have fun at times, but it's not a vacation.

CHAPTER 13

SPEAKING AND LISTENING

Speaking and listening are two important parts of the communication skill set that are essential for any leader. This chapter presents suggestions for effective speaking, the *sending* piece, and listening, the *receiving* piece, to help a leader evaluate and improve each of the skills. Pick and choose what might be helpful, starting with speaking.

> "*How* you speak is as important as *what* you say."

Speaking

Speaking is perhaps the most straightforward way information and ideas are transmitted. And it is the means that a leader uses to influence, persuade and direct. Being a good speaker is an important skill, but not the only one, needed to be an effective leader. Chances are you already speak reasonably well to be where you are. Nevertheless, let's examine characteristics of effective speaking with the intention of identifying a nugget or two you can use to improve your speaking style.

First off, there are ethics associated with speaking.[49] They include:

- **Having something to say:** saying something of substance; otherwise, don't waste another person's time. Those around you don't need more noise.[50]
- **Being prepared:** You have an obligation to be prepared, know what you're talking about, and present whatever you have to say in an organized manner.[51]
- **Being truthful:** Speak the truth and don't shade, bend, or misrepresent it.[52] It's okay to state what you believe to be true and why. Where there are differences of opinion, alternatives or a dispute as to what the facts are, say so.
- **Being honorable:** Be honorable in your motivation. Do not deliberately mislead, misguide or misrepresent yourself or your subject matter to manipulate the audience's understanding with false information or nefarious intentions.
- **Giving credit to your sources:** Do not plagiarize other people's ideas or words in part or whole.
- **Being civil:** Do not insult, berate or denigrate an individual or group about their race, religion, gender, sexual orientation, right to free speech, or holding opposing views. At the same time, it is acceptable to argue, disagree, debate and make a case for or against, so long as it is done in a civil manner.[53]

Successful Speaking

The following points are basic to successful speaking. Many are statements of the obvious. They may not make you a captivating, charismatic or brilliant speaker, but if applied, they will put you on solid ground for making your point or accomplishing your purpose.

- Speak from the heart. Sounds corny, but it's true. If you know what you're talking about and believe it, your sincerity will come through loud and clear. At the same time, realize that people have good instincts for what is sincere, coming from within, and what is not.

- Along the same line, be enthusiastic, upbeat or positive in your presentation and demeanor. Enthusiasm creates a positive environment for a fair hearing. Also, it's contagious. But don't try to fake it. Even if you are not a polished speaker, sincerity and enthusiasm can overshadow other flaws. Audiences are forgiving and receptive if they perceive you are sincere and giving it your best.

- Being nervous about speaking in front of a group is normal for most people.[54] A measure of it is even good, encouraging diligent preparation. Nervousness can be managed by several methods, including:

  o Thinking positively. Look at speaking as an opportunity to share good ideas.

  o Preparing well. For some people, it might help to write a verbatim manuscript (a word-for-word script) and read it aloud several times. Writing down what you want to say forces you to organize your thoughts and think about selecting the right words and phrases, and it develops familiarity, confidence and a rhythm.

  o Visualizing yourself giving a successful presentation. Imagining yourself delivering your talk or speech exactly as you want it to go is a mental exercise. Go through it mentally, beginning to end, over and over again. Performers and athletes use visualization as a mental rehearsal all the time.

     o   If appropriate, using visuals. Audience attention will be drawn *to* the visual and *away* from you, relieving you of being their visual focal point.

     o   Seeking opportunities to speak, not avoiding them. The more you speak, the better you'll get. With this realization, your confidence will grow.

- Speak on subjects you know about. It's easier, and you do a better job.[55] What you don't know, research. If there is another person better qualified or more knowledgeable on a subject, introduce that person to speak. You owe your audience the best you have, and that might be someone else.

- Speak *with* your audience, not *at* them. Whether the receiver of your words is a single person, a small group, or a large audience, approach it as a conversation. It's friendlier and more palpable.

- Approach speaking from your audience's perspective.[56] Spend time analyzing your audience, their level of knowledge on the subject, and their interests, and gear it to them. Ask yourself, "Why do they want or need to hear what I have to say?" Give your audience a reason or motivation to listen to what you have to say. Refer to chapter 4, "Your Audiences," for a more in-depth discussion of the importance of knowing your audience.

- Don't talk too long or to fill time. If you do, your audience will find their own distractions or tune out, and you'll never know. They will still be there physically but in a different place mentally. Speak as long as you must to accomplish your purpose and no longer.

- Speak with *purpose*.[57] "My purpose in speaking to you today is …" is blunt and not very elegant but a good way to begin. It leaves no doubt. You don't want your audience wondering,

"And the point is?" Not only is this frustrating for your listeners, but it undermines people's regard for you as a leader.

- Organize your presentation in a logical manner to help your audience to follow along and understand what you are attempting to convey. Have a clear introduction, key points of your talk, and a conclusion, each with transitions or signals, as you move from point to point.[58] Outline of a simplistic example:
  - o Introduction: "Good morning! Today I am going to talk about three market trends that are affecting our sales. It's important to all of us because ..."
  - o Transition to first point: "The first trend is ..."
  - o Transition to second point: "The second trend is ..."
  - o Transition to third point: "Finally, the third is ..."
  - o Transition to conclusion: "To recap ... I hope you see how these three trends are affecting our business and what we need to do to ..."
- Storytelling is a good technique for delivering a message or making a point. It stimulates listeners' imagination, entertains, adds a little drama, humanizes something that may be dry, abstract or theoretical, and supports your point. Including a good story is an effective technique for capturing attention and advancing your argument.[59]
- Humor is also a good technique for gaining attention and entertaining. But humor can also be a double-edged sword. If it goes well, your audience is entertained and amused, and it sets a favorable tone for the rest of your presentation. If it falls flat, people don't get it, or it is offensive or controversial, it can undermine your purpose and reputation. Know the makeup of your audience and proceed with caution when incorporating humor.

If you're planning to use humor, it might be a good idea to try it out on someone else, a trusted colleague, to see if it works.

- Speechwriters: If you are a very busy person and have the luxury of a speechwriter or a person on staff (from Communications?) who can help you prepare remarks or a presentation, be sure to give that person sufficient time and guidance about your intended message and points or details you want to address. In addition, schedule reviews to enable the presentation to evolve from a concept to an outline to a working draft to a finished piece, be it talking points or a full-scale script and visuals.

- Be pleasant and smile, especially at the beginning and end of a talk. It's a good way to begin any conversation and encourages your audience to listen with a positive attitude. Yes, business is serious, and leaders are paid to identify, address, and solve issues. We tend to focus on the negative—things that need to be fixed or problems that need a solution. Even when bad news and unpleasant matters must be addressed, find something to comment on that is going well or someone who is doing a particularly good job. As a minimum, thank your audience for their time and attention, and their dedication to the task at hand. "We're all in this together" is a good theme for a beginning or ending.

- After you are finished speaking, linger for a few minutes, allowing members of your audience the opportunity to approach you with a question or comment. Be approachable. And lingering afterward may give you some initial feedback as to what resonated with listeners.

Visuals

Visuals—slides, graphics, illustrations, video—can be helpful in a speaking situation. Your words working together with a good visual can make it easier or clearer for your audience to understand an idea or concept. Hearing and seeing—involving two senses—helps some people comprehend better than just hearing. Visuals can also be distractions if they don't complement or illustrate what you are saying, attempt to cover too much, or are too complicated. If you use visuals, follow these guidelines:

- Say what is important about each. Clearly state why you are showing this visual or what you want your audience to see or understand.
- Make sure the words and illustrations are large enough and readable for everyone in the room.
- Use key words and bullet phrases—not sentences.
- Limit phrases to three to five words and bullets to no more than four or five points.
- Don't read visuals to your audience—elaborate on keywords and bullet points, using them as talking prompts.
- Show extracts, callouts or highlights if it is necessary to show a complicated spreadsheet, flow chart, decision tree or wire diagram.
- Talk about the visual as soon as it comes up and take it down when you have finished addressing it.
- Face and talk to your audience, not to the visual.
- Don't attempt to dazzle your audience with visuals that are spectacular works of art. You can overdo it, and the amount work required is not worth the benefit derived. A simple slide or visual is often good enough.

- Don't be guilty of death by PowerPoint. We've all sat through too many PowerPoint presentations. Another can be a turn-off or cause your audience to tune out.

Persuasion

Leaders speak for many reasons: to inform, introduce, congratulate, report, motivate and persuade. Perhaps the most challenging function, and the one most often required of leaders, is speaking to persuade. Persuasion requires evidence or proof. Don't underestimate your audience. Physically, they sit there courteously and listen. Mentally, they are having an internal conversation, weighing what you are saying. Based on your credibility and evidence, they agree or disagree, are swayed or not, are motivated or not. Credibility is other people's faith and trust in you based on your position, demonstrated knowledge, and prior history, and it's earned over time. Evidence is more tangible and requires proof. Tools for persuading include:

- **Examples** in the form of stories or case studies of similar circumstances and outcomes, making a situation real and helping people draw parallels.[60]
- **Testimony** is the word or recommendation of recognized experts or individuals whom you and your audience know and trust for what you are proposing.[61]
- **Statistics and numbers** quantify and make a strong case for a proposal or argument. Even so, numbers need to be explained because they can be confusing or manipulated. Spreadsheets with too many lines, columns, and numbers—too much information—can be counterproductive. Go easy with stats and numbers, using only what you must to make your point.[62]

- **Reason** relies on logic and clear thinking to arrive at a conclusion that your audience can follow and agree with.
- **Emotion** depends on evoking visceral feelings for an often-predictable reaction and can be a powerful influencer. Like statistics and numbers, using only an emotional appeal to make your case is to be on thin ice. It's okay for a pep talk, but it's questionable and weak as the sole basis for decisions or matters of importance.

Delivery Situations

How you speak is as important as *what* you have to say. Poise, stage presence, preparation, message, organization, confidence, voice, eye contact, posture, body language and dress can all figure into the total package of how effective you are as a speaker. Also, situations are different and dictate your method of delivery. As a leader, you should be able and prepared for *impromptu, extemporaneous,* and *scripted* speaking situations.

- **Impromptu Speaking** is speaking with little or no preparation. As a leader, you will find it often happens that you are asked to "say a few words" without prior warning.[63] Don't shy away from these pop-up opportunities. Unless you are responding to a specific question or situation, have a hip-pocket talk always ready that you can adapt to any audience, circumstance and time constraint on a moment's notice. Bend and shape it to fit the situation. Build a hip-pocket talk around a favorite or timeless topic or theme. Topics that lend themselves to hip-pocket talks include:

o Teamwork: we depend on each other, and we're in this together.

o No matter where you are in the organization, your job is important.

o You represent our company every time you speak to a customer.

o No matter what you do, do it right the first time.

- **Speaking extemporaneously** is speaking from memory, with occasional glances at notes—if you can. By doing so, you make a better connection with your audience. It assumes you know your subject matter very well, are well rehearsed, and appear confident.[64] Speaking extemporaneously allows you to move around and maintain eye contact with your audience. They will pay closer attention with the reaction, "The boss really knows his or her stuff."

- **Reading a manuscript** makes sure you cover what is important and in a logical manner. It may be necessary and appropriate when precision is important, such as when making promises, stating policy, or making statements that have legal consequences.[65] Do your best to read your script in a manner that sounds natural, varies in volume and emphasis, and pauses in the right places. Try to vary pace, and avoid speaking in a monotone. Even when reading, look at your audience from time-to-time to stay connected. Use techniques, such as underlining, capitalizing, highlighting, symbols, or margin notes as prompts to help you moderate your delivery.[66]

Listening

Listening is the other part of communicating that doesn't get the attention that speaking gets; yet, it is just as important. A lot of knowledge, information, intelligence and opportunities are missed because of poor listening.[67]

Listening is harder than people realize. Obstacles to effective listening are hard to overcome. One is the discipline, or lack thereof, to resist distractions, especially the cell phone or iPad. Also, it can be hard to remain objective when preconceived notions and biases are confronted and challenged. Finally, attention spans vary from person to person and, for many of us, are not long enough to remain focused for more than a few minutes.

Techniques for improving listening skills include:

> "A lot of knowledge, information, intelligence and opportunities is missed because of poor listening."

- Take listening seriously, and commit to work at it.[68]
- Resist distractions, whether they be external noise, visual, or mental.[69]
- Don't prejudge the speaker based on appearance, accent, ability as a speaker, position or other differences.[70]
- Listen to the speaker's entire presentation or argument—consider all points.
- Listen for evidence—examples, testimony, statistics—in other words, *substance*.[71]
- Take notes—listen for and write down salient points, evidence, arguments, key words and phrases, and questions.[72]
- Quiz yourself—immediately afterward ask yourself, "What did I just hear? What was important? How did the speaker explain or support his or her ideas?"

Finally, listen with sincerity. People have a need to feel heard. You show respect by listening attentively and indicating you have heard not only their words, but also the intent and feeling behind the words. A simple "I hear you" or repeating the words the other person used are techniques for providing feedback that you have listened and understood.

Our world has become a circus of sights and sounds—many devices and platforms, all kinds of noise, music, drama and controversy at every turn, sound effects, voice-overs, fast-moving and captivating video and animation, and crawl lines at the bottom of screens, besides what's going on in our heads—all combining to create information and sensory overload. It's hard to concentrate, discriminate and think. It takes determination, discipline and a commitment to listen and sort through what's important and relevant.

Leader's Takeaway

- Your effectiveness as a leader is shaped largely by how well you speak and present yourself. Speak from the heart on subjects you know about, consider your audience, and prepare well. The more you speak, the better you'll get.
- Too much is missed due to poor listening. Being a good listener is harder than many of us realize. Leaders can improve their listening skills, but it takes commitment, discipline and practice.

CHAPTER 14

CRISIS COMMUNICATIONS

It's easy to be a leader when everything is going well. However, your leadership and often your character are tested when things go wrong, whether it's a minor hiccup or a crisis. This chapter addresses communications considerations and actions when things go wrong. Like it or not, bad things happen in organizations, just as they do in most people's personal lives. As unpleasant as it is to consider what can go wrong—what can seriously damage your organization physically, financially, its reputation, and your personal effectiveness as a leader—you must plan

> "Are you ready for a crisis? It's not a question of *if,* but rather *when* one will occur."

for accidents and incidents and have contingency plans in place to guide your actions. Dealing with an emergency or crisis is particularly challenging because when things go terribly wrong, initial information is sketchy at best, the actual situation is often not clear, and emotions interfere with level-headed thinking, making a leader's role difficult and unnerving. Nevertheless, the negative effects can be significantly reduced by how a leader reacts and communicates.

There are many case studies and a large body of knowledge on crisis management from which to draw lessons. Our purpose here is to get you thinking about your responsibilities and point you in the right direction so that you and your staff can fulfill your responsibilities, not *if,* but *when* a crisis occurs. Consider what is presented here, and tailor it to your situation.

People First

It is difficult to predict or even imagine all the things that can go wrong; yet, you, with the help of your staff, have a responsibility to consider likely possibilities and develop contingencies to manage the risks. No matter what goes wrong, there are a few fundamental principles that should always guide your actions.

- In order, protect people first. The safety of people—your subordinates, workers, the public at large, anyone and everyone in your sphere of influence—is your first and most important responsibility.[73] Then, do your best to protect property and resources, whether they are yours or someone else's.
- Act quickly. Often minutes, even seconds, are critical in emergency and crisis situations. Don't allow yourself to become paralyzed by the situation. Act, and act quickly.
- Do not hesitate or delay in notifying the fire department, police, EMTs and others, including your superiors or headquarters, even with incomplete information. Get the response ball rolling.

- Do not cover up, deny, delay, or minimize the reporting of bad news. Report it as completely, honestly and quickly as you can to proper authorities.

What Could Possibly Happen?

Recognize that a crisis can take many forms, each with different effects and consequences, each requiring thoughtful consideration, and each demanding action. They might be any of the following:

- Mother Nature induced: tornadoes, hurricanes, earthquakes, snow or ice storms, floods
- Physical or mechanical: power outage, plumbing problems, fire, explosion, laboratory incident, computer system failure
- Human related: medical, legal, workplace violence, misconduct, misappropriation, fraud, discrimination, accusation or claim, damaging news that is true or false
- Business related: economic downturn, competition, product failure, product recall, lawsuit, strike, facility closing, layoff
- Other external causes: traffic or an emergency nearby affecting your operation, spillover from political, economic, terrorist, war, refugee, and other extreme events

All are possible, with some being more likely than others. Each is very different, but all have an impact on your organization, represent an interruption in your operation, and require you and your staff to react to mitigate or fix the situation. Some events you will be able to manage; others you can only react to.

Team Effort

Although you as a leader have primary responsibility, dealing with a crisis is a team effort.[74] The size of the team depends on the size of your organization, the nature of your business, and associated risks. Whatever your business is, designate a crisis management team for planning, responding, and following up afterwards. You, the leader, should head up the team. In no particular order, Human Relations, Security, Legal, Facilities, Engineering, Operations, and Communications—in other words, your primary staff—form the core of your crisis team, with the addition of whomever else you think is needed. If it makes sense, add others with special knowledge or experience. If you have a safety officer, a medical doctor or nurse, and a business continuity manager, include them on the core crisis management team. If you are a small organization, you might invite outsiders with experience in specialty areas to help in planning.

Take a Before, During and After Approach

The *before, during* and *after* approach is a good way to attack the process of crisis management.

Before

- Prior planning for crises is essential. Cobbling together a response on the fly as an emergency or crisis unfolds is unacceptable and negligent, with potential legal consequences.[75] Having a response framework in place with identified players, responsibilities, contact lists, contingency plans, and checklists is a good start and demonstrates proactive and caring leadership. Be involved in the planning. If you delegate it, make time to review the plan in detail with key members of your team. You don't want to be reading a response plan for the first time as you are facing a live crisis. It's not a good time for a first look!

- Dedicate time for risk assessment and crisis planning. Annual business planning sessions or retreats are ideal opportunities. Insist that the right people are present and participate. Granted, it is painful to dedicate time to potential crisis situations that you hope and pray will never happen, but it's not wasted time. It is more painful to be caught without a plan or with an outdated one.

- Planning and risk assessment should lead you to preventive measures. Identify, correct or fix dangerous situations *before* they result in an incident.[76]

- If emergency plans already exist, use the time for a detailed reading, review and update with key players. Resist rubber-stamping them year after year without a careful review. Too many changes occur.

- Beyond your internal crisis management team, consider including others—outsiders—for planning for special situations and for expertise and resources you lack and they have. These might be your local fire department, police, hazmat, EMT, medical unit, and heavy or specialized equipment operators. Due to their expertise and experience, they may be helpful in identifying gaps you and your staff have overlooked. Also, seeking their input during planning creates an opportunity to meet them, establishes a working relationship, and familiarizes them with your operation should their services ever be needed.

- Once crisis plans exist, make sure people know about them. Not everyone needs to know everything, but everyone does need to know his or her role for a given situation. Keeping employees informed of proper actions to take should be a collaborative responsibility of Human Resources and Employee Communications. Methods might include:
  o briefing new employees during orientation
  o giving every employee a wallet-size laminated card with instructions on what to do if xyz occurs
  o having prewritten internal/intranet and social media messages containing instructions ready for mass notification at a moment's notice[77]
  o having an intranet page dedicated to contingency actions for review by employees at any time[78]
  o instituting a certification requirement that employees must review or pass annually, reinforcing their knowledge of actions to take in certain situations
  o in case of an electronic systems failure, having posters, infographics, and signs with instructions in breakrooms and on bulletin boards
- For quick reference, leaders should have crisis folders or three-ring binders (hard copies) on a nearby shelf or at their desks with plans and instructions of actions to take for given situations.
- Conduct periodic drills, rehearsals, and tabletop exercises (full-scale and abbreviated) for evacuations, shelter in place, decontamination, mass casualty and other responses to likely

scenarios, and document them. Drills and rehearsals uncover deficiencies, holes and coordination disconnects.[79]

- Hold a *safety day* annually. Use it to review plans, remind people of proper actions to take, conduct drills or rehearsals, and inspect or clean up workplaces where potential hazards may exist. If there has been a string of accidents or injuries, conduct a *safety stand-down* in which all operations come to a halt and everyone in the organization focuses on safety, prevention and corrective actions.

- When addressing employees in various forums, use the opportunity to remind employees of proper responses to emergency situations. If a crisis event has occurred in another department, facility or company, talk about its relevancy to your circumstances and how your organization might have reacted.

- Establish a "dark" website or section or page of your intranet listing actions to be taken when a crisis occurs.[80] Your Information Technology people can quickly unmask or activate the dark site when a crisis occurs, giving employees instructions about what to do.

- Checklists are an excellent tool for leaders and staff, making sure each pays attention to critical tasks during an emergency.

- Designate primary and backup systems for communications—wired, wireless, even messengers.[81]

- Designate a primary and backup official spokesperson.[82] That should be you and your Communications director. Make it clear to all concerned who is authorized to speak for the organization and to whom all inquiries should be referred.

- Direct Communications to monitor traditional and social media channels for indications or warnings of a potential crisis.[83]

- Establish a deep chain of authority designating who is in charge without a doubt in case you are not present or available—your number two, number three, number four, number five, etc.

During

- Act to protect or ensure the safety of people.
- Notify first responders—fire department, police, medical authorities, others as appropriate.
- Notify superiors.
- Activate your crisis management team and plan. Have a crisis management command post and position yourself or a member of your leadership team at the scene of the crisis with a communication channel between the two.
- Account for the people for whom you are responsible. Know their location and disposition. Have designated assembly or rally locations.
- Have someone designated to record information—the time, who reports what, other details—to have an accurate record of the crisis as it is happening.
- Be visible to employees and subordinates. They need to see leaders responding appropriately. At the same time, position yourself at the scene of the incident or at the crisis command post—wherever you can do the most good.
- Remain calm and level-headed. Your actions, directions and body language communicate that you are in charge and doing what a leader should be doing at such a time.

- Coordinate and communicate with key players and superiors frequently. During crisis situations, there is a thirst for information. Satisfy it with frequent updates or situation reports, even if the update message is "no change." Often in emergency situations, especially early on, information is spotty, sometimes inaccurate, and fragmented because it is reported by different sources. Record it all. A clearer picture of the actual situation will begin to emerge.
- If the situation warrants, be prepared to hold a news conference or make a statement to the media.
  - o If you don't communicate with the media, they will still report on your crisis from whatever they see or can gather, and from whoever will speak with them.
  - o By talking with the media, you establish yourself or your designated spokesperson as the source for official information and control the flow of information.
  - o An advantage to holding a news conference is that all media get the same information at the same time.
- In answering media questions:
  - o Remain professional, controlled and calm.
  - o Take responsibility, don't make excuses, and remain focused on actions to take care of people and limit further harm or damage. There will plenty of time after the emergency or crisis is resolved and order restored to pick apart what happened and determine why it happened and who or what was responsible. The immediate concern is that a proper authority—a leader—is in charge and bringing the situation under control.

- o Acknowledge and talk only about the facts—what has occurred and what is being done to mitigate the crisis. Correct erroneous information.

- o Do not speculate on or theorize what might have been the cause. Do not allow reporters to suggest or put words in your mouth. It's okay to say, "I don't know" or "We are looking into that—I'll tell you when I know."[84]

- o If there are casualties, express concern and empathy for them early on in your statement and say what is being done to take care of them and their families.

- o Be careful to protect the privacy of casualties and follow proper procedures for the notification to their family members.

- o Don't linger after the facts are out and reasonable questions answered. Remove yourself from the presence of media.

- o Promise and deliver updates if the situation warrants.

- Social media is going to be alive and buzzing with activity during a crisis.[85]

  - o Make social media work for you. Use it to issue instructions and collect information.

  - o Issue authoritative statements about the facts of the situation as known, describe what is being done, and avoid speculation.

  - o Monitor social media channels during a crisis to gauge how people are reacting, collect information, and correct false or speculative information.[86]

After

- Conduct a review or evaluation of what occurred and actions taken in response, and assess the damage. Be honest, objective and critical.
- If warranted, direct that an investigation be initiated to determine the circumstances that led to the situation. If an outside proper authority investigates, pledge and provide support and cooperation.
- Use traditional and social media channels to invite internal and external responders, participants, stakeholders, and witnesses to submit their observations and recommendations.[87]
- Make changes to emergency response plans based on *lessons learned*.
- Report and make a record of after-action findings, results and changes to superiors and participants that have a vested interest in what occurred. Include a list of steps to respond to or preclude another occurrence.

Being a leader in a crisis is an uncomfortable place to be. But it can also represent an opportunity. If you handle it well—with decisive leadership, a good plan, coolheadedness, a good staff, people knowing what they are supposed to do and doing it, compassion, and priorities in order—then the respect people have for you and your organization can be significantly enhanced. But responding well to a crisis doesn't happen automatically. It is the result of recognition of its importance, serious and realistic planning by a lot of people, practicing, refining, updating and briefing people—all at your insistence. Crisis planning is another case of "If it is important to the boss, subordinates know it, and magically, it's important to them!" Let them know crisis management is important to you.

Leader's Takeaway

- Good leadership counts most when things go wrong. When a crisis occurs, subordinates expect their leaders to be decisive, visible, level-headed, taking charge and leading from the front or wherever the emergency is.
- Crises happen all the time. It's not a question of *if*; it's more a question of *when*. A big part of crisis management is planning and communicating effectively.
- The *before*, *during* and *after* approach is a good model for planning. Developing checklists for each phase and function ensures all critical tasks are addressed.
- As a leader, you have a responsibility to anticipate and plan for *before* a crisis, take charge *during*, and implement corrective action *after*. If you delegate planning, satisfy yourself that acceptable plans are in place and you know what they are.

ENDNOTES

1   Sam Deep and Lyle Sussman, *Smart Moves for People in Charge* (Reading, Massachusetts: Addison Wesley Publishing Company, 1995), 1.

2   Ibid., 263.

3   Ibid., 35.

4   Ibid., 93.

5   Ibid., 117

6   Dan O'Hair, Gustav W. Friedrich, Lynda Dee Dixon, *Strategic Communication in Business and the Professions* (Boston: Pearson, 2016), 20.

7   Stephen E. Lucas, *The Art of Public Speaking* (New York, The McGraw-Hill Companies, Inc., 2012), 18.

8   Carol Kinsey Goman, *The Silent Language of Leaders* (Hoboken, New Jersey: John Wiley and Sons, 2011), 1.

9   Ibid., 3.

10 Ibid., 21.

11 Allan and Barbara Pease, *The Definitive Book of Body Language* (New York: Bantam Dell, 2004), 21.

12 Goman, op. cit., 29.

13 Pease and Pease, op.cit., 123.

14 Goman, op. cit., 23.

15 Goman, op. cit., 63

16 Goman, op. cit. 26.

17 Pease and Pease, op. cit., 71

18 Goman, op. cit., 103.

19 Goman, op. cit., 43.

20 Goman, op. cit., 49.

21 Goman, op. cit., 46.

22 Goman, op. cit., 49

23 Pease and Pease, op. cit., 32.

24 Pease and Pease, op. cit., 38–39.

25 Pease and Pease, op. cit., 65.

26 Goman, op. cit., 111–112.

27 Pease and Pease, op. cit., 23.

28 Lucas, op. cit., 98.

29 Lucas, op cit., 113.

30 Deep, op. cit., 1.

31 Deep, op. cit., 198.

32 Antony Young, *Brand Media Strategy,* second edition (New York: Palgrave MacMillan, 2014), 49.

33 O'Hair, Friedrich, Dixon, op. cit., 20.

34 W. Timothy Coombs, *Ongoing Crisis Communication,* fourth edition (Thousand Oaks, California: SAGE Publications, Inc., 2015), 101.

35 Deep, op. cit., 105.

36 Deep, op. cit., 20.

37 Deep, op. cit., 53.

38 Deep, op. cit., 59.

39 Deep, op. cit., 56.

40 Deep, op. cit., 58.

41 Deep, op. cit., 57.

42 Deep, op. cit., 14.

43 David Meerman Scott, *The New Rules of Marketing and PR* (Hoboken, New Jersey: John Wiley and Sons, 2015), 55–56.

44 Dave Kerpen, *Likeable Social Media* (New York: McGraw-Hill, 2011), 6.

45 Young, *op. cit.,* 40–41.

46 Kerpen, *op. cit.,* 46–47.

47 Robert W. Bly, *Advertising Manager's Handbook* (Englewood Cliffs, New Jersey: Prentice Hall, 1993), 116–124.

48 *Ibid.*, 124–129.

49 Lucas, *op. cit.*, 30–31.

50 Chris Anderson, *TED Talks* (Boston: Houghton Mifflin Harcourt, 2016), 24–25

51 Lucas, *op. cit.*, 32–33.

52 Lucas, *op. cit.*, 33.

53 Lucas, *op. cit.*, 34–35.

54 Lucas, *op. cit.*, 9–16.

55 Lucas, *op. cit.*, 78.

56 Deep, *op. cit.*, 43

57 Lucas, *op. cit.*, 82.

58 Lucas, *op. cit.*, 66–67.

59 Anderson, *op. cit.*, 64

60 Lucas, *op. cit.*, 142.

61 Lucas, *op. cit.*, 155.

62 Lucas, *op. cit.*, 147.

63 Lucas, *op cit.*, 241–242.

64 Lucas, *op. cit.*, 242–243.

65 Lucas, *op. cit.*, 241.

66 Lucas, *op. cit.*, 216.

67 Kerpen, *op. cit.*, 14–15.

68 Lucas, *op. cit.*, 53.

69 Lucas, *op. cit.*, 55.

70 Lucas, *op. cit.*, 56.

71 Lucas, *op. cit.*, 57.

72 Lucas, *op. cit.*, 58.

73 Coombs, *op. cit.*, 139.

74 Coombs, *op. cit.*, 68–70.

75 Coombs, *op. cit.*, 15.

76 Coombs, *op. cit.*, 38–40.

77 Coombs, *op. cit.*, 186.

78 Coombs, *op. cit.*, 103.

79   Coombs, *op. cit.*, 75–77.

80   Coombs, *op. cit.*, 186.

81   Coombs, *op. cit.*, 101.

82   Coombs, *op. cit.*, 80.

83   Coombs, *op. cit.*, 26.

84   Coombs, *op. cit.*, 84, 132.

85   Coombs, *op. cit.*, 95.

86   Coombs, *op. cit.*, 157.

87   Coombs, *op. cit.*, 163.

BIBLIOGRAPHY

Anderson, Chris. *TED Talks*. Boston: Houghton Mifflin Harcourt, 2016.

Bly, Robert W. *Advertising Manager's Handbook*. Englewood Cliffs, New Jersey: Prentice Hall, 1993.

Coombs, W. Timothy. *Ongoing Crisis Communication,* fourth edition. Thousand Oaks, California: SAGE Publications, Inc., 2015.

Deep, Sam, and Lyle Sussman. *Smart Moves for People in Charge*. Reading, Massachusetts: Addison-Wesley Publishing Company, 1995.

Goman, Carol Kinsey. *The Silent Language of Leaders*. Hoboken, New Jersey: John Wiley and Sons, 2011.

Kirpan, Dave. *Likeable Social Media*. New York: McGraw-Hill, 2011.

Lucas, Stephen E. *The Art of Public Speaking*. New York: The McGraw-Hill Companies, Inc., 2012.

O'Hair, Dan, Gustav W. Friedrich, and Lynda Dee Dixon. *Strategic Communication in Business and the Professions.* Boston: Pearson, 2016.

Pease, Allan and Barbara Pease. *The Definitive Book of Body Language.* New York: Bantam Dell, 2004.

Scott, David Merman. *The New Rules of Marketing and PR.* Hoboken, New Jersey: John Wiley and Sons, 2015.

Young, Antony. *Brand Media Strategy,* second edition. New York: Palgrave MacMillan, 2014.

www.ingramcontent.com/pod-product-compliance
Lightning Source LLC
Chambersburg PA
CBHW032002170526
45157CB00002B/510